MY LIFE CHANGIN

By Lucy Reynolds

With Dan Alborough

To Tosh
Who made me who I am today.

© Lucy Reynolds 2009
First published 2009

All rights reserved. No part of this publication may be reproduced, in any form or by any means, without the prior consent of the author.

ISBN 9780900616 85 3

Printed and published by
Geo. R. Reeve Ltd., 9-11 Town Green, Wymondham, Norfolk

# CONTENTS

| | |
|---|---:|
| Acknowledgements | 4 |
| My Life Changing Moment | 5 |
| Chapter Two | 12 |
| Chapter Three | 14 |
| Chapter Four | 19 |
| Chapter Five | 23 |
| Chapter Six | 27 |
| Chapter Seven | 33 |
| Chapter Eight | 38 |
| Chapter Nine | 41 |
| Chapter Ten | 44 |
| Chapter Eleven | 47 |
| Chapter Twelve | 54 |
| Chapter Thirteen | 59 |
| Chapter Fourteen | 64 |
| Chapter Fifteen | 69 |
| Chapter Sixteen | 73 |
| Chapter Seventeen | 76 |
| Chapter Eighteen | 80 |
| Chapter Nineteen | 83 |
| Chapter Twenty | 89 |
| Chapter Twenty One | 94 |
| Chapter Twenty Two | 98 |
| Chapter Twenty Three | 105 |

# ACKNOWLEDGEMENTS

So many people have helped, supported and loved me during the writing of this book. The words, thoughts and feelings in this book are mine alone. I did not intend to upset or offend anyone. I have been on an emotional rollercoaster and many have joined me on this journey.

Firstly I need to thank Dan. He has been extremely patient. When I started the first few words, I sent them to Dan. He encouraged me to continue writing, he questioned me, bringing out more thoughts and memories that had slipped into the remote corners of my mind. He helped shape the book you are reading today. Without Dan's help this book would never have been published.

Thanks go to Jason Wightman, a talented Graphic Designer, who created the cover for the book you're reading now. His skill and flair will no doubt have caught your eye already!

I also need to thank Dad and Mum (Fred and Joyce Reynolds) for their continued love. I know I have not been the model daughter and have caused them much hurt and sadness. Hopefully as time has gone on, this has changed to pride and happiness. I am blessed with parents who love me despite everything.

Peter and Katherine Ireland have accepted me in their lives and the more time I spend with them, I realise how lucky I am to have them in my life.

Bramwell and Marlene Sheens and their family have shared their lives and their home with me. I have been welcomed as a part of their family at some of the most private family moments. I am grateful for their continued love and support.

I was so lucky the day Vanessa Comer was sent to my door. Her compassion and friendship has helped me so much. She made me feel safe at some of my most unstable moments. She is an exceptional human being.

Finally I have to thank Val Waterman and her family. Val has been my most valued friend for over 10 years. In all my endeavours she has never judged or lectured me. When the policeman knocked on my door in November 2005, my thoughts of who to call went immediately to Val and she did not let me down. Her home is like my second home and her family treat me as one of their own. I can't thank them enough.

# MY LIFE CHANGING MOMENT

Most people talk of life changing moments but I know exactly when mine was. My life changed beyond recognition on Sunday 13th November 2005 at approximately 13.45. I heard a knock at the outside door of our flat. I went downstairs to answer it. I was cursing my better half, thinking he had mislaid his keys. Knowing Tosh, this would never have been the case but my mind did not register this at the time. I got half way down the stairs and saw through the window a car parked in our parking space. The car was white and covered with blue and yellow luminous squares. On the roof was a metal bar containing a blue strip of light, my mind told me this was not our lilac/blue Ford Escort but I did not connect the car with what was about to happen..

I answered the door and there stood the biggest, largest policeman I have ever seen. He completely filled the doorway with his height and his build. I can't remember exactly what his words were, but he was basically asking 'Does Darrell Sheens live at this address?' Darrell Sheens was Tosh's real name. 'Yes', I replied, 'but he is not here at the moment', 'Does he drive a Ford Escort registration number N615 CWA?' 'Yes', I replied again. He asked if he could come in for a minute, because there had been an accident. Not knowing what else to say, I motioned 'Yes, of course, come in.'

We both lumped up the stairs and entered the living room. He asked if I was alone and when I said yes, he asked if there was someone I could call. I thought of my only friend apart from Tosh and went to call Val. I was on auto pilot by this time. The policeman was extremely patient with me (I am sorry I can't recall his name). He allowed me to ramble on complete drivel whilst wandering from the living room to the kitchen to call my friend. The policeman had explained there had been an accident with our car and a train but he did not expand on the details. I did not think to ask more at the time. Val was out shopping and so I went on my computer, clicked on the Yellow Pages website and found the telephone number of the supermarket where she shops. Staff at Customer Services proceeded to put a customer call out, but Val did not appear. I put the phone down and then returned to the living room in a complete daze. I have no idea how I was able to go on the internet and find the number and call but I guess it was an automatic thing to do at the time. It seemed like hours but it must have been a matter of minutes when Val called me back. I told her there had been an accident with Tosh, our car and a train and could she come over. She said she would be there as soon as she could.

In the meantime, there was another knock at the door and the policeman went to answer it. It was another member of the Constabulary, this time a female and she introduced herself as PC Vanessa Comer. She came in, guided me to the sofa and sat me down. She held my hand and, in the kindest way she could, she told me that the man I had spent my life with for almost sixteen years had died, when his car was struck by a train on the level crossing at Swainsthorpe, the next village along from where we lived. That must be a difficult thing to have to do, to walk into someone's home not knowing who will be there, or how they are going to react to hearing the news that someone they loved had died.

Vanessa was patient and caring. She asked if I had someone I could call and I said my friend was on her way. Val arrived and I just blurted it out 'Oh Val, Tosh is dead.' We both hugged and cried. The first policeman expressed his condolences and checked with Vanessa if he was still needed and he then left. Vanessa remained, hugging and holding me. She asked if I was ok and if there was anyone else who needed to be informed. She was talking about relatives. Tosh and I had lived for almost sixteen years alone, without contact with either of our families. I realised that despite the choices we made during his life, his family had a right to know their son had died.

Vanessa took down the details I could remember of his parents, i.e. their names and the last known address I could remember for them. As Tosh was forty-five and the youngest child, I knew they were not going to be young and I was not sure of their health or well being. I explained my concerns to Vanessa, who rang through to Police Headquarters and began the search for Tosh's parents. Policemen were dispatched to break the hearts of another family. Whatever Tosh's thoughts and his reasons for being apart from the family, only he can say, but I am sure he would not have wished to cause such pain and heartache as he did on this day.

Both Val and Vanessa let me be myself. I could hug, hold hands and cry and at no point was I made to feel I had to put on a brave face. I think I did not really let go of my emotions until I was alone but I feel that was due to shock and not knowing how to react to the situation I had been flung into. I had never thought of Tosh dying, or anyone dying for that matter. This was a new and steep learning curve for me.

Vanessa told me that information and details would be released soon and it was my choice how I wanted to be told this information. I had three options.

1 – To be told things as they happened.

2 – To be told things after they had happened.

3 – To be told everything that could happen, even if it may not ever become actual fact.

I chose the third option, to be told everything. I felt if I knew what was happening, or likely to happen, I could be prepared. I had no idea what I would be told, or how I was to be told it at this time.

Vanessa explained she had been the second officer at the scene of the accident and that due to the impact Tosh would have been killed instantly. She asked me when I had last spoken to him.

I explained it had been our normal Sunday routine. That morning, after washing our new bedding and hanging it out to dry, Tosh had gone to the supermarket to do our weekly grocery shop and he had left me to finish my dressmaking. He had telephoned me from the car park of the supermarket to check if it was raining, where I was and could I keep a check on the washing? He told me it was raining where he was, only fifteen minutes by car. Cursing him for not trusting me to pay attention, I went downstairs to check on the washing. It was blowing in the breeze and bathed in sunshine. I did not trust my own instincts and was worried I would let him down by forgetting to check the weather, so I'd brought the laundry in and continued my sewing.

Tosh arrived home and put the shopping away. I did at the time question why he had bought so many stock items. Tosh was a very methodical person and liked the cupboards to be fully stocked, always buying a replacement item before we got to the penultimate tin or packet. On his final shop he filled the cupboards with pasta, tuna, longlife milk, beetroot and cereal. He brushed my question away, by explaining that there was a special offer on at the moment.

Thinking about it much later, I realised he knew I was going to have no transport to shop for heavy items, as he was going to destroy our car by taking his journey onto the level crossing.

I am amazed how calm he seemed in hindsight, still thinking and planning ahead when he knew he was not going to be around to help me any longer.

He said he still needed to go back for petrol, because the queues were too long and he wanted to get the frozen food home. Tosh mentioned there were a few other bits he needed to do and that we would go out for a ride later when he got back. We kissed and he told me he loved me and I told him the same, as usual, and he was gone.

He had added that he would give me time to finish sewing. I was making a black skirt for work and black thread is difficult to sew, unless it's daylight. He had sent me a text message just before 13:00, "Hi Hon, be back at 14.30". I had just replied back "OK". The next thing I knew was the knock on the door by the policeman.

Vanessa said she needed to take the name of his dentist and a comb or toothbrush for DNA. I was not needed to identify his body. The crash meant that dental records and DNA would do this for me. Vanessa took down the details of his dentist and put his toothbrush in a clear plastic bag. She put my mobile phone in another plastic bag and promised to return it to me in a few days time. Tosh had suffered from depression in the last couple of months and I gave Vanessa the prescription he had never cashed in for antidepressants. He had only said that morning that he was going back to the doctor the next day to ask for some counselling, as we could no longer cope alone without some expert help. He had not mentioned suicide and I had not thought of the word or its meaning before.

Vanessa said I should not be left alone. Val said I should come back with her as I had no one else and I would be alone. I tried to argue, saying I would be fine, but Vanessa agreed with Val and it was two against one. They helped me pack a few things and Val only lived about five miles away so I could come back if I needed to stay longer to pick up more items. Val gave Vanessa her address and phone number and Vanessa gave me her mobile number. She told me that number was mine to use whenever I needed her. It would be on twenty four hours a day, seven days a week. She explained she would be my contact to liaise with the British Transport Police, who would investigate the accident. Vanessa became my Family Liaison Officer, or FLO. My mind was frazzled! Why would I need to be in contact with the police? I don't know what I would have done without Val and Vanessa. I have very vague memories of that move, from life with Tosh to staying with Val. The first few hours just blended into one another.

I was in shock, but I did not know it at the time. Everything had happened so suddenly. It was like I was on auto pilot. I was answering the questions Vanessa was asking me and not really understanding the true sense of what was happening to me. I had heard the words, "Tosh is dead", but I had no real understanding of what that meant. I was numb and just kept repeating myself. The same phrases were being said again and again. "I can't believe this has happened", "Tosh is dead". Vanessa had only met me a couple of hours earlier; she must have had a weird picture of me. She did not question my ramblings but continued to listen, talk and hold my hand to reassure me I was not alone and that she was there for me.

I remember she also spoke to Val and told her if she had any worries or questions just to get in contact. We collected my overnight bag and went back downstairs together and, with a final hug, Vanessa then left to continue her duties and I went home with Val. I spent the rest of the day in a daze. Vanessa called me later in the evening to check on me. Val had her son, Glenn, staying with her at the time so I slept on the floor under a spare duvet as her spare room had Glenn in it. Val's son and her husband David both made me so welcome.

I had been friends with Val for over ten years and during that time I had got to know her husband David and both her children, Deborah and Glenn. Both Deborah and Glenn are a few years older than me and their lives had taken them away from the area. Both of them had always made me welcome and often said I was their unofficial adopted sister. During the years I had known Val, I had happy memories of spending time with her family. Val's mum lived in the next street and her door was always open, she wanted to share what Val and I were up to and where we were going. Sadly, Grace died in October 2007. Grace was a wonderful lady, who was not afraid to speak her mind if she had something to say. She had great stories and tales to tell. It was funny to hear Val being told off by her mum when she was doing something wrong. You could always tell when Grace was giving her a telling off, because Val changed to Valerie. She was a terrific lady and is greatly missed by all of us.

Tosh and David became friends through my friendship with Val. David and Tosh both shared a love of horseracing and gambling in general. Tosh had learnt how to play Poker from David and it was a game he excelled at and enjoyed right until his death. Without the support of Val and her family that day I don't know what would have happened to me. Shock did begin to kick in later in the day, but I was feeling numb. I kept thinking this is not really happening to me. Tosh could not really be dead….but he was.

People have asked me, how did I feel when I heard the news that Tosh had died? I have to be honest, it was just words, it felt unreal. It was like I was in a daydream. I felt I would wake up and it would be something we would laugh about together… but that never happened. I did not dream it.

Val took me home and gave me cups of tea and lots of hugs and allowed me the freedom to ramble about the terrible thing that had happened. I totally disrupted her life. The normal Sunday routine was thrown out of the window when I arrived to stay with her. I had no concept of time, or being hungry or thirsty. I was hot then shaking with cold, it was shock. It must have been a shock to Val too, she had been my closest friend for so long. Not many people got to know Tosh but Val and David both knew him, through the trials and adventures we had survived over the years. Val and Glenn were to help me so much in the next few weeks. I was lucky Glenn was at home with Val for a holiday at the time, as he let me cry, laugh, hug and talk when Val needed a break from my rambling. Glenn is like the big brother I never had and we are still close to this day. We have both helped each other a lot over the years. Our closeness remains, even when we don't see each other as often as we would like.

At the time my life changed forever, Val's life was turned upside down too in those first few hours and days. There were phone calls to be made and answered. Visits from Vanessa, which meant a police car outside, for neighbours to question and gossip about what could be happening. During all this upheaval Val never complained. She reacted as any loyal and trusted friend should, with love, hugs and lots of patience.

Any death is terrible, but the sudden death of someone so young is a shock. What will I do without him? That was the ultimate question and I had no idea of an answer at the time.

I don't think it really registered what was happening until bedtime. We all took turns in the bathroom, then one by one, said goodnight. It was then that it hit me, as I lay on the floor of Val's back room where only a few hours before we had been drinking tea and sharing a meal. Reality hit me that, although I had people around me, I was totally alone. Val was wonderful, but the person I needed to talk to was no longer here. In the nights that followed, I talked to Tosh out loud. Lying alone on the floor in the dark and in unfamiliar surroundings I cried my hot, salty tears, and asked him, 'Why did you do this to us?' These times were my time alone to let my emotions flow. It was not a conscious thing that I held it together during the daylight hours and went to pieces when I was alone in the dark. I slept a little, but the questions I had no answers to returned to jolt me awake and remind me why I was not in my warm bed with Tosh any longer.

# CHAPTER TWO

I could not really believe Tosh was no longer going to be around. My life for the past fifteen plus years had been totally Tosh. My first thoughts were how could he do this to us?

We met soon after my twenty-first birthday. My cousin took me and my twin sister out for a birthday drink with some of his friends to celebrate our milestone. We enjoyed the evening and were invited to join them again - and it became a regular Friday night thing. Everyone would meet at the local pub for a first drink, then when everyone was assembled we would bundle into cars and drive to a quiet village pub to drink, play pool and play music on the jukebox. My lasting memories of those Friday nights were playing pool and eating steak sandwiches late into the night.

My sister took her friend along and the three of us girls paired up with three of the lads to play pool. The girls were pretty rubbish, so the boys' shots were just to correct our mistakes. I was paired with a chap called John and sometimes with Tosh. It was always just lots of fun, pure and simple. My sister was always paired with the same chap who, quite a few years later, became her husband.

At the time we were just enjoying the company. I remember the jukebox always played Thin Lizzy's 'Whisky in the Jar', but I can't remember any of the other songs that were played. I quite fancied the shy chap John, but he never asked me for a date and I was not brave enough to ask him. Then one night Tosh asked John, 'are you going to ask her out?' John went scarlet and muttered something shyly. Then Tosh came over and asked if I would like a lift home. This was his way of asking me out, as he did not have a car at the time! He lived in Norwich at the time (nine miles from my hometown of Wymondham) and he relied on his friends to pick him up so he could still join the gang for a drink. Many evenings he was forgotten, often John had forgotten he had promised to pick him up and one night they were both stranded when John's Morris Marina broke down.

I digress. After Tosh had asked me out, I drove him home and I never looked back. Our first official date was a month before his thirtieth birthday in March 1990. He was working as a licenced bookmaker at the greyhound track in Great Yarmouth, taking bets on evening horseracing as this was in the days before betting shops opened in the evenings. The more time we spent together the closer we got and decided to buy a plot of land and move into a caravan on the plot in November 1990. From that moment we had just each other in all the adventures and traumas that followed. After all we had been through together, how could I survive alone now?

It had only been a matter of hours, but already my life had changed. Tosh had been the stable part of my life, through good times and bad. I felt alone, shocked, confused and very numb. I was breathing and thinking on auto pilot. I was staying at Val's house and my entire world felt strange and unfamiliar, like living in a fog. I could not think what to eat, or when to drink. It was a most unusual situation to find myself in to say the least...

# CHAPTER THREE

The following day, Vanessa contacted me again to see how I was and to tell me Tosh's parents had also been given a FLO and through him they had asked if I would go and meet them, as they would love to meet up with me. Vanessa and the other FLO arranged a meeting for the next day. On the Monday evening, I telephoned my parents for the first time in fifteen years to explain what had happened. I spoke to my Dad and then my Mum and arranged to go and see them after meeting Tosh's family. It was a very emotional conversation. The next day was going to be a tough one for all of us. I was about to meet Tosh's family, who had lost a son they would never see again and be reunited with my parents, who were getting their daughter back.

Tosh's details had been kept confidential from the media. The local television and newspaper just said a man in his forties had died, when his car was struck by a train at a level crossing. I had to let my family and Tosh's family know what had happened before his name was released. I had called in sick from work and they were all shocked to know it was Tosh that had died. People were so kind at this point and I was told if there was anything they could do, to just call the office. They told me to take as much time off as I needed and not to worry about work at all.

I was anxious about meeting Tosh's family. It must have been a hard decision for them to invite me into their home and into their lives. They had just lost a son they had not seen for around fifteen years, but they were going to meet the girl he had chosen to share his life with, while excluding them. I was lucky, Vanessa said I did not have to meet them if I really did not want to, but I had done nothing wrong and thought it might help all of us. Their FLO had told her they were keen to see me. Without a car, I had no idea how I was going to get there. I didn't want to bother Val, she had done so much for me already! However, Vanessa said it was not a problem, I would not be going alone as she would be coming with me.

She arrived the next morning in an unmarked police car and she was dressed in plain clothes. This struck me at the time as thoughtful, not to be in uniform and without the highly visible car, which might cause the family more distress.

I was very nervous, but I was in good hands. Vanessa told me she would not leave me and that if it got too uncomfortable then she would bring me home. During my life with Tosh I had not had any friends, except Tosh himself and Val, so I was quite uncomfortable making small talk with people I knew, never mind strangers. I had never felt uncomfortable with Val or Vanessa. If there was a pause in the conversation, it was not a problem.

We arrived at the house and Vanessa squeezed my hand, asking if I was alright. I nodded and I took a deep breath and we walked up the drive. We were welcomed at the door by a very emotional group. Lots of hugs and tears were exchanged, before we went into the living room. I was introduced to everyone and I introduced Vanessa. I sat on the sofa with Tosh's sister Sue, his parents, their FLO and Vanessa completed the group. Vanessa sat opposite me and her eye contact reminded me I was not alone and amongst friends.

Tosh's family made me welcome and I did my best to tell them how we had lived the past nigh on sixteen years. During our time together we had moved nineteen times. We never quite had enough funds to buy the house of our dreams, so we bought, sold, renovated and built from scratch trying to make a better life for ourselves.

At one point, we lived in Spain and had more adventures renovating our home there, when the floors collapsed after four to six weeks of moving in. All the time, I was filling in the gaps of Tosh's life that his family had missed out on. I am not sure I would have been as kind as they were to me that day, if our roles were reversed. It must have taken a lot to hear about the life of your son or brother from someone who would be a constant reminder of the man you lost. Tosh's life was in two parts, the first thirty years with his family and the last fifteen plus years with me. That first meeting was to put the two parts together. Vanessa disappeared into the background and kept us supplied with cups of tea. It was nice to know she was around and close by. Tosh's brother, Stephen, had been missing from that first meeting as he was working but I was told that he did want to meet me, if I would be happy to come back another time.

After several hours, I needed to leave the family to make my next emotional reunion. Sue volunteered to drive me to my Mum and Dad's house, so Vanessa could be released back to her normal duties instead of being my taxi! We hugged and she said her phone was still on if I needed her and we would speak later.

Sue drove me to my parents' home and on the way she thanked me for being so open. She said it had really helped her and her parents to know something of the life I had shared with her brother and that he had been happy and enjoyed a full life. I was an emotional jelly at this point. I had discovered I am fine if someone is indifferent to me, but the moment someone is kind or nice to me it makes me tearful. I was dropped at my parents' house and we arranged a time for her to come back for me.

I walked up to my parents' front door, not certain of what emotions would surface. Dad just opened the door and hugged me. We were all in tears. Then Mum hugged me and told me 'Welcome home. This will always be your home, whatever happens to you.' We sat and talked and cried and hugged and Mum said she had prayed for a day we would be in touch again, but never thought it would be in these circumstances. I told them both that I couldn't change the past, only the future and we agreed to start from now and not revisit old hurts. I know I have hurt my family in the past and in doing so I have also hurt myself. However, to have regrets over the life I chose would soil the happy times I shared with Tosh. If our life together had not just been the two of us I don't think we would have had the great life experiences we did together, so I have few regrets. I just never intended to hurt so many people that cared for me so deeply.

My life with Tosh had been so different. Cutting ourselves off from both families made us closer. When I look back now, I can see lots of good points and quite a few bad points to living the life we lived.

On the positive side we were free to live the life we chose. If we had friends and family to consider, we would not have lived the nomadic life that we began leading. Moving house gave us so many challenges and adventures that taught us both to rely on each other, making us quite self sufficient and also insular. Having only ourselves to worry about gave us the freedom to live abroad and for Tosh to pursue his love of gambling and poker. If we'd had the influence of families and friends, I am sure we would have been persuaded this was not the normal way to earn a living, even though it was perfectly legal and - in Tosh's case - very enjoyable. I am certain we would have been urged to live a more conventional lifestyle.

When I think back now, about the way we chose to live, I don't think it was that healthy to cut ourselves off from most of society, which included family and friends. As a teenager I was extremely shy and lacked confidence. I went to London when I left college, to work as a children's nanny, and I gained an enormous amount of self-confidence. When I met Tosh, my self-confidence was on the up and my shyness was diminishing. Once we ceased contact with our families, Tosh became the dominant person in my life - and in the beginning the only person in my life. My concern about displeasing him meant my self-confidence became eroded over time.

After fifteen years of being dominated by Tosh, I found I had no friends except Val and that my social skills were nil. I was unable to hold a conversation with anyone, even work colleagues, for fear of saying the wrong thing. I could not make small talk beyond talking about the weather. If I had stayed in contact with my family I believe I would have seen sooner that the life I was living was not healthy.

Tosh was not a religious person and, although he never stopped me or told me I was not to go to church, I did not feel able to continue attending. During my time in Sunday school, then church youth club and church for as long as I could remember, I was always taught the importance of marriage and the whole life I was living with Tosh went against all that I had been taught was right. So I stopped going to church. However, if I had continued attending a church, or place of worship, I would have had contact with people and this would have helped my social skills.

These are things I cannot change, as they made me and Tosh who we were, and the life was much more memorable for it. This being said, I am also aware now that through our selfish actions of splitting from both families, we caused numerous hurts for both sides. Every Christmas, birthday, wedding and birth that happened whilst we were living our lives apart would have been a constant hurt to our families, as we were not there to share them.

Tosh is no longer here to say what he feels about it, but I deeply regret the hurt and sadness I brought to my family.

During my time with my parents, I filled in my missing years and we drank a toast with Dad's homemade apple wine to "happier times". They told me that my sisters had both got married, that my twin had two children and both of them would love to meet up as soon as possible. The time went so quickly and my lift arrived to take me back to the next reunion. I left my parents, carrying a couple of bottles of homemade wine to give to Tosh's family. The rest of the evening was spent meeting Stephen and his wife, Annette, recalling the stories of the missing years. I wanted Tosh's family to know he had been happy in his life and had achieved many of his dreams. I had no idea how I would cope without him. It sounds dramatic, but that was how I felt.

By the time I got back to Val's house later that evening, I was physically and emotionally drained.

# CHAPTER FOUR

I began looking back on my happier memories. Some of our happier moments in our life together were when we had time away from the pressures of the reality of everyday life. Due to Tosh's dominant personality, it was only when we "checked out" of everyday normal life that this happened.

One of these times was spent on the small island of Formentera. We had decided we needed a break, so went to the travel agent and booked a last minute allocation on arrival, somewhere warm. When we got to the airport, we were told we had been allocated a half board holiday in Formentera. Tosh was a terrible air traveller; he was so scared of flying. We had tried to plan for Tosh's phobia and in preparation he had taught me to play Cribbage. The idea was that we would play cards to distract him from his fear. I was an excellent pupil and the ruse worked, enabling Tosh to fly with limited fear.

The flight was delayed leaving Norwich. It was a most surreal day, with it being the day of Princess Diana's funeral. We drove to the airport with no traffic problems as the roads were deserted. We checked in and went through to the departure lounge. Usually the departure lounge was light hearted with people happy and laughing, eager to be going on holiday. Today was completely different, the mood was sombre and all the television screens were showing the procession of Princess Diana's coffin through the streets of London, towards Westminster Abbey, for the service. Everyone was quietly watching the screens, or reading the newspapers which were also blanket coverage of the Princess' death. The whole country had been hit by a state of shock and grief. There was only occasional interruption, with the call of flights ready, for passengers to board the various departures from the airport.

Our flight was to the island of Ibiza and from there we were to catch the ferry to the tiny island of Formentera. As our flight from Norwich had been delayed, we were rushed through to catch the last ferry of the day. We boarded the ferry with our bags and cases, looking forward to a relaxing break. As the ferry left Ibiza, we were treated to a wonderful sunset. Deep colours of red, orange and pink lit up the sky.

On our arrival we were told that is was too late for our evening meal, as the kitchen had closed. However, a platter of meats and cheeses were set aside for us, along with fresh bread and crackers and a bottle of red wine to welcome us to the Hotel Cala Sona. Our room was basic but clean. No television or radio, or contact with the outside world. At this time we were not part of the mobile phone age (we thought they would never catch on), so had fourteen nights of no contact with anyone.

The first morning we went down to breakfast, which was buffet style and a relaxed affair. We then went for a walk to explore our home for the next two weeks. The hotel was directly on the beach and, apart from a small shop and a shed with cycle hire, there was very little there. The hotel at the time was family run and English was spoken by the younger members of the family only.. and this was broken English. I had a few Spanish phrases and a dictionary to get us through.

After a relaxing day on the beach, we discovered that the peaceful and isolated location of the hotel meant the beach was used by nudists. We did not have a problem with this lifestyle and thought "Why not?" We found the feeling of the sun directly on your skin felt like you were warm right through to your bones. It was such a liberating feeling and stripped naked you felt more equal to the others sharing the beach. To swim in the sea without clothes was such a wonderful feeling and the weightlessness and the feeling of water touching my skin made me feel glowing and alive.

The only time we needed to dress was for meals. Breakfast was an informal affair and shorts and beach clothes were more than acceptable. The evening meal was the event of the evening in the hotel. Without any bars or restaurants within walking distance, guests tended to remain in the hotel. There were no distractions like television, making for a more relaxing atmosphere for drinks on the terrace, followed by the evening meal.

The evenings followed a pattern of showering and dressing for dinner, then enjoying cocktails on the terrace. As we did not hire a car, because the island was so small, drinking and driving was not an issue for us. A large cocktail, complete with cardboard parrot for decoration, became the ideal start to the evening. This gave us a chance to chat to other couples who were staying at the hotel, or to enjoy the setting sun on the terrace overlooking the sea. The evening meals were also buffet style and of an extremely high standard.

We'd often wile away the time out on the terrace chatting to the other holiday makers, or playing cards, board games, or reading from the extensive bookshelves in the lounge area. One evening we were entertained by some local dancers in traditional costume. However, most evenings were a relaxed affair.

After a couple of days relaxing on the beach, we decided to explore the island. We bought a map and hired a couple of mountain bikes and armed with a rucksack, bottles of water, fresh bread and cheeses and fresh fruit we set off each day to see other parts of the island. There was very little traffic so cycling was not a problem and we soon found some lovely out of the way coves to enjoy the sunshine and the sea. The cycling gave us exercise and we felt healthy and relaxed. Tosh's character was also visibly more laid back and he became less dominant, as we shared the basic decisions of the day. Choosing which direction to cycle to and when to stop and share lunch. We laughed and loved and enjoyed our time away from reality.

Being away from all forms of reality, we both became more easygoing and it was like the first few months of being a couple again - before the responsibilities of day-to-day life had kicked in and brought some stress and worry to our lives.

It was around this time that we were thinking of leaving England for good and making a new life abroad. It was a wonderful dream, to think we could feel like this forever.

We had three places in mind. The first was Ireland, mainly because the language was the same and the gambling aspect was there in the form of greyhounds and horseracing. We had been to Ireland for holidays, but eventually discounted it due to the changeable weather. To have the Emerald Isle remain green you needed lots of rain, so the weather would be a bit too much like home!

The second choice was Biloxi, on the Gulf Coast of the USA, in the State of Mississippi. This town had sand, sea and casinos, they spoke English and the housing was affordable. The one thing against the idea was the distance and the cost of flights. Flights to America at this time were expensive and there were no direct flights to that area. With hindsight it was the right decision, because in August 2005 Hurricane Katrina swept through the area and Biloxi was destroyed in her wake. The area is being rebuilt and regenerated as I write.

The third choice was Spain. Enjoying the trappings of the Spanish island of Formentera, we decided Spain was where we would plan to move, so our Spanish dream would begin there...

To arrive at this destination, most tourists go to Ibiza and take the boat to Formentera, but we did it the other way round. The only excursion we took during that fortnight was "an evening in Ibiza town".

It was a very different evening for us. A lovely meal in a restaurant in the old town before the new part began to fill with party goers. I don't remember seeing so much leather or items of torture since visiting the London Dungeons! Men dressed as women and vice versa. Some were being whipped and tied in leather. It was not my kind of thing and we were both relieved to be back on the ferry and to our peaceful island retreat.

Our trip to Formentera was the last relaxing time I remember spending with Tosh. We had a few of those moments in our lives, where we walked along the beaches of Lanzarote much later in our life together, but that particular fortnight spent doing nothing slowly was a wonderful happy memory that will stay with me always. Further holidays were spent house hunting on the Costa del Sol and the Costa Blanca, so not really holidays at all, more like working trips. Chasing around the Spanish coast line looking at houses with no roofs or walls, requiring some updating, or plots of land without any electricity or water supply was not the relaxing beach holiday we often needed! We eventually found our Spanish home via a contact we met at York racecourse, where else?

# CHAPTER FIVE

In September 2000 we sold all our possessions and left England, to make a new life for ourselves in Spain. We had purchased a three bedroom town house in a place called Carib Playa, on the Costa Del Sol. The plan was for this to be our retirement home. We were looking for a slower pace of life and to take in a different culture and lifestyle. We had enough money saved to pay the mortgage for five years, in case it was not possible for us to find work to support ourselves.

Tosh found a job in Gibraltar within a few weeks, working for the bookmaker Stan James. Travelling to Gibraltar took one and a half to two hours each way so Tosh worked three long days to reduce the number of journeys, but maintain the hours for the income.

I found a job selling timeshare holidays, or 'Holiday Club' as they liked to be known as. I was appalling at selling, I was much too soft. After months of stress and worry I was offered a non-commission based job in the office, booking Russian clients and sorting out their visas for travel. This was a fixed wage which proved to be a safer option for me, as my selling was so poor. I did manage to sell enough (before being offered the other job) to buy groceries, but not much else. The office and administration post suited me (and my employer!) far better.

Just as we were beginning to adjust to our new lives our house decided to collapse around us. When we arrived we discovered the furniture had termites. Sometimes, while sitting quietly in the evenings, we could literally hear them munching through our wooden furniture. We were scared of losing the stairs and door frames, so we removed all the furniture to prevent the spread of these hungry creatures. We bought a plastic table and chairs, with the thought that these could be used on the patio at a later date when the situation was resolved. Also, as an extra bonus, termites can't eat plastic!

No sooner had we removed the termite situation, we discovered a problem with the floors. The house was thirty years old and the floors had been laid in the traditional Spanish way – a layer of sand, a layer of cement and then finally the tiles were placed on top. Over the years the sand had dried out and disappeared, leaving a gap between the floor and the tiles. As we began to live in the house, the tiles dropped into the gap. As the floors were interlocking, the whole house had to be renovated.

As our home would need to be completely gutted and rebuilt, we decided that it was the right time to put in a new bathroom and sanitary ware. We also planned to redesigned the kitchen. To decide where to connect the waste pipes, we needed to see which manhole our waste went into. As we were experienced renovators, we used the age old trick of flushing the toilet and looking down the manholes to see where the coloured pieces of paper appeared, as we flushed them through our system. Many flushes followed and all the available manholes were looked into, without results. It turned out our house was not connected to the mains! In fact, it was not connected to anything and the waste was just flushing into the ground! We got the Spanish version of "Dyno Rod" and with the help of a German neighbour, who acted as a translator for us, this was confirmed and our waste was sucked up and taken away. This proved a great source of interest and entertainment to the local Spanish residents. The smell of thirty years of waste was horrendous. The kitchen was made into a makeshift toilet so the waste pipe could be put straight through the wall and into the main drain until the renovations were completed.

We then needed to somehow put the house back together, but our money was being eaten away fast! Our first Christmas in Spain was spent rewiring the whole house, not quite how we imagined it to be. Tosh was an approved electrician and I was his labourer. We then got quotes from three builders to renovate the house, because this job was too big for us to take on ourselves in a foreign country. The cheapest quote was from the German builder, the middle level quote was from the Spanish builder and the most expensive quote was from the English builder.

We decided to go for the middle ground and opted for the Spanish builder. Explaining that we had only had enough money to renovate either upstairs or downstairs, not both, he said 'No mi amigos, todo'. We explained we did not have the money to do it all (todo). He replied that it was not a problem. You pay what you can and pay the balance when you have money. We got our German neighbour to explain again, he said he understood but it was too expensive in the long run to do only half the project and that he would be happy to wait for the money. We weren't totally comfortable with this set up, but as he came with good recommendations from people in the area, we agreed and the work began.

I have to say, the workmanship was fantastic. They arrived at 8.00am and left at 7.00pm, with only a half hour break in the day. There was no question of "Manana". We had heard of stories that Spanish builders would not work long hours or not turn up when they say, or disappear once the job had been started but we never experienced this during the whole job. To keep the costs down we had gutted the place, so they were just rebuilding. When it was finished it was beautiful and the builders could not be faulted for the time they spent on site or the quality of their work. Ironically, they put the floors back the same way - a layer of sand, a layer of cement and then finally the tiles on top.

Once it was finished we knew we had to sell it to pay off the remaining debt to the builder, so we put the signs up in Spanish and English to sell the property. Selling property in Spain does not involve the near-necessity of using an agent like we do in the UK. One of the downsides to this was that we had many time wasters (well, even more than you'd expect!). The Spanish that visited treated it as a family day out, with mother, father, sons, daughters, uncles, aunts and grandparents all viewing the property and tutting and muttering at the price the English were selling their property for.

It was in April 2001, when most of Europe were preparing to change currency to the Euro and many German and Irish property purchasers came to search for deals in Spain. Some had money that they did not wish to declare. Money to be changed into Euros had to be traceable and proof was required to track its source and in some cases this was not possible, we were told, so many properties were bought at this time with untraceable money.

Fortunately, timing was on our side and an Irish man came and viewed our property and fell in love with it. It was a short stroll to the beach in a quiet Spanish area, so it was easy to see its appeal. After all, it was why we had bought it in the first place.

The property was sold and we stayed in Spain in a rented apartment whilst trying to decide on our future. Val and David came and stayed with us for a holiday and we had some lovely evenings out for meals in local restaurants by the beach, as well as some pleasant time people watching in Puerto Banus and feeding the fish in Puerto Cabopino. They reciprocated and we came to Norwich for a holiday with Val and David, before returning to Spain once more.

On 11th September 2001 the world changed for many people. We were living and working in Spain and had no English television and were trying to make sense in our basic Spanish of the news reports and pictures of the Twin Towers in New York. Once the terrible news began to unfold it became clear, in any language, the world we knew was changing forever. We stopped and took a fresh look at our lives.

The idea to move to Spain was to enjoy a slower pace of life and the outdoor life we could not enjoy in England. We loved the romantic walks on the beach after work, also the mountain biking and swimming in the sea and outside pools. To enjoy meals and a beer alfresco was another plus. However, we were not having enough time after work to learn Spanish, to integrate with the Spanish people. I had made friends with a Spanish lady living near Malaga through my love of Cliff Richard, but somehow it wasn't enough. Tosh and I felt we really did not have the time to learn the language properly, or to take in the culture. We did not want to live as stereotypical "Brits abroad", so we decided to return to England and begin again.

Living abroad in a country where we knew no-one was a wonderful experience and we both said we would never regret the decision to try it. If we had been in contact with our families or had children of our own that experience would not have been possible, or tricky at the very least. I was always the cautious one and with Tosh's itchy feet and Romany spirit I got the opportunity to experience a life I would not have been brave enough to try alone.

I could not believe my brave adventurer had died. What would my life be like without him?

# CHAPTER SIX

Deciding to return to England was the easy bit. We were returning to a very different country and had no idea life was going to be so expensive. Living in Spain our rates were only minimal, we had no telephone or satellite television. Spain had no council tax or television licence. The car tax was paid to the local council and used to upgrade the roads in your local area and food and drink was very cheap. So much so that eating out had become an everyday occurrence.

We flew back to Norwich airport to be met by Val, who had bravely agreed to let us stay in her spare bedroom until we got ourselves settled.

With no jobs, no home and no transport, our lives were in a suitcase and two rucksacks. The only item of value was Tosh's tool box. He hated being an electrician, but had agreed to work using this skill if we needed it. The day after we got back, I called the temporary staff agency at Norfolk County Council to register for work. I had worked for them before and they were happy to have me back. I am certain the whole world is based on the theory of it's not what you know but who you know. I was informed my faxed CV and reference had arrived and, as I had worked on the register before, they could offer me work straight away. Being offered three week's work starting on the Monday, I took it immediately. After all, I had no other way of earning a living and it would help to get my foot in the door for more regular work.

We spent the weekend scanning the newspapers and shop windows for homes to rent. Val had assured us that we could stay with her for as long as we wanted, but we did not want to outstay our welcome and ruin a wonderful friendship. Having a two week holiday or spending a day or an evening was one thing, but to move in for an unspecified time can put a strain on even the best friendships. Tosh was not someone who was happy or comfortable taking a helping hand in any form, so he found this very difficult.

Monday morning arrived and I presented myself at County Hall for my first day back at work. Familiar faces passed me and one lady stopped in reception and said "hello" and carried on past me. She then returned ten minutes later and asked if I was Lucy. I said I was and she started to laugh. Explaining that she was told to go and get Lucy from reception that was starting work again today, it turned out that she was thinking of someone else. After this mix up was explained, I was given the job of entering timesheets on the pay system for supply teachers. Apparently, another Lucy had been doing this previously, but had gone back to university to complete her studies. I was not the Lucy they thought they had asked for! I told them I had been offered three weeks full time work and I was ready to work, even if I was the wrong Lucy.

I was shown what to do and the three weeks were extended. Then I was asked if I was happy to help out paying adult education tutors. I had no problems with working and they were happy with my work, so one contract linked to another and I eventually had a permanent, full time contract in HR doing payroll and contracts. I have had continuous service since returning from Spain in October 2001. I still don't know what job I want to do, but the job is a challenge, as the rules and regulations change, and it pays the mortgage and the bills!

Meanwhile, whilst I was working, Tosh had a hard task ahead of him to find us somewhere to live. He found a terraced house just off Unthank Road in Norwich. Within three weeks of being back in the country, we were in home of our own. Tosh was busy buying crockery, glasses, towels, duvets and pillows etc. to make our house more of a home. We still did not have our own car or a television but managed without both these for about twelve months. Living in the city centre, we were able to walk most places anyway, or use the buses. Most evenings were spent reading books or newspapers and listening to the radio.

During our time at Val's, Tosh and David had become good friends and their shared love of all aspects of gambling helped pass the days and nights during our stay there.

David enjoys playing Poker, a game Tosh had not got around to learning and it was not long before David taught Tosh how to play. They spent many evenings discussing the rules and objects of 'Texas hold 'em' and seven card stud. David lent Tosh books on the game and within a few months he was hooked. He was a very controlled gambler and always gambled with his own money. Anytime he lost, he absorbed the loss and when he won I got a share or a present of my choice. It was usually a new bike or a weekend away, nothing too over the top – but very welcome all the same!

Tosh loved the game, because in Poker you could sit down at the table and play anyone in the world and have an equal chance. In no other sport could you play against the world champion if you were new to the game and have a chance at winning. Poker is a game of bluff. You are dealt cards and by betting you can make your opponents believe you are holding a better hand than you actually are. Most players who are great at the game give nothing away in emotions, body language or in facial expressions. That's where the term "Poker Face" comes from. Tosh was very good at this and proved to be very successful.

We began rebuilding our lives and soon realised that if we were going to buy a property we would need to do so very soon, as property prices were rising faster than our incomes, despite both of us working full time.

I was now in HR with a permanent contract and Tosh was working in Trading Standards at the council, as a Trading Standards Officer. He enjoyed that job because it was not office based and he could plan his own visits and not have to do the regular nine-five hours. He hated being office bound so that job suited him.

We bought a house in Martham, near the broads just twelve months after returning to England. We remained friends with Val and David but had no other friends apart from them. After all the time that had passed we gave no thought to making contact with our families. It had been over ten years since seeing them and although my sister Katherine was only working ten minutes down the road from my office, our paths never crossed. After so many years, you tend to forget the reasons why you ceased contact in the first place and we no longer wondered if those reasons were still valid. Added to that, pride kicks in, so that you will not allow yourself to get in contact, too much water under the bridge. At least, this is how it felt at that time.

Tosh's job situation changed when he began to give serious consideration to the fact that he might be able to earn more money for less time while enjoying playing Poker. We sat down and discussed the pros and cons of giving up salaried work to play Poker and decided he should give it a go. He was always meticulous about money and budgets. He wrote out a budget plan of how much we needed to bring into the home to live and pay the bills. We worked out how much both of us needed to bring into the house by whatever means. I told him that as long as our standard of living did not drop and that I was not to be the only one bringing home a wage, he could give it a go. He promised to bring in his share by whatever means possible, even if he had to dip into his personal savings. We had a joint account, and then we gave each other a weekly allowance we called 'sweetie' money to use how we wished. Tosh's sweetie money seemed to be growing by the minute as it was speculated on stocks and shares and spread betting. My sweetie money was spent in cinemas, theatres and live music concerts. Anything left over was put into our own personal savings accounts, so the housekeeping account was never in danger from a bad turn of the cards or a slump in the stock market.

This way of financing our life was to continue until his death. Poker was a new form of gambling in England at the time and due to television coverage of a few tournaments, it soon took the world by storm. Tosh would spend his time playing live Poker games in casinos, with David and their friend Alfonso (sadly no longer with us). The trio began playing in Great Yarmouth, Brighton, London, Luton and Walsall. On some of the trips I would accompany Tosh and we would make a weekend of it. We would go to the casino, I would watch him begin playing and then escape to a local cinema, or a London show, or live music at the NEC in Birmingham. I also enjoyed quite a few evenings at a theatre in Wolverhampton. The weekends were always funded by Poker winnings. This was a side of gambling that most gamblers would not recognise, Tosh decided that if he was winning that we should enjoy the freedom it gave us, so life did not pass us by. He was aware from past experience of being a bookmaker how quickly a winning streak could end and the pattern of losing take over. He was not a stereotypical gambler, as he saw this as a way of earning money doing something he enjoyed, rather than just winning.

As with everything Tosh did, he did it to the full. When he was playing Poker, we ate, slept and breathed it. I never considered not joining him in his passion. Looking back now, I can see that this was another form of obsessive behaviour on his part. When he was not playing live games in a casino, he was watching live and recorded tournaments on the television.

There were also magazines, books and of course the internet.

I also got caught up in the Poker revolution. So I could understand the jargon and winning hands, Tosh taught me how to play. I began to understand the buzz of being dealt 'pocket aces' or 'two snowmen', and the excitement and panic of going 'all in'. I had played poker at home, but never wanted to go out and play a live game in a casino. Always happy to people watch and understand how the game is played, I was more at home on the roulette table. Tosh liked the etiquette of Poker and the casino atmosphere, but hated the smoke-filled rooms he had to play in. Poker took off on the internet in a big way. The large bookmakers understood there was money to be made from internet gaming and Tosh signed up for tournaments online. His online name was 'Rosemary'. It confused fellow players because men and women tend to play Poker very differently. As he logged on with a female name, his fellow players were put off balance when his card play was different to what they were expecting. Some tournaments were long, six to eight hours in most cases and players would begin to get tired and make mistakes. Tosh was happy to wait and when he saw an opportunity he would make a move. So he could take a break to eat a meal or take a bath, I would sit in for him. This would confuse the other players even more, because Rosemary would begin to play Poker in another very different way. I did not have the patience to wait, and tended to play every hand dealt, hoping to get lucky. I was quite successful and Tosh would often take his seat back at the computer to more Poker chips than when he left it. On the occasions that I had lost chips he was never cross with me but seemed to brush it off, saying "it's just a game".

One of the prizes for winning a tournament was a place in another higher level contest and from this on to a place in the live Poker game, The Northern Ireland Open. Tosh won his place and, with all expenses paid, he jetted off to Belfast. I returned to the airport to pick him up two days later. He was so happy and elated, because he had been placed twenty fifth out of over a hundred and fifty players - winning five hundred pounds for his trouble. I still have a DVD of him playing that tournament and you can see him happy, relaxed and chatting to his fellow players.

Doing so well in that gave him the confidence to take on bigger and better opponents. The biggest tournament in the World is the World Series of Poker, held in Las Vegas. It was played in Binions Horseshoe, a casino in downtown Las Vegas. It was and is every poker player's dream to play in this tournament. The entrance fee is steep, so the casino includes early rounds via satellite to win a place in the starting line up.

Even the greatest players take part in these tournaments hoping to win a place without having to pay the $10,000 entry fee. In 2007, the winner of the World Series of Poker defeated 6,358 players to win over $8 million and a gold bracelet. Binions tradition was to give the winner this gold bracelet and this tradition still continues today.

Tosh never wanted to pay $10,000 to play for ten to fourteen days solid, but the Worldwide satellite rounds gave him the opportunity to play against the best on the planet.

We shared three holidays in Las Vegas and I could not have been more proud to see my man playing at the Poker table with the World number one and World number two ranked players, holding his own and enjoying the banter. All three holidays were paid for with Poker winnings including flights, hotel, food and entertainment. Who says gambling does not pay?!

## CHAPTER SEVEN

Over the first few days after Tosh's death, I spent many hours with Tosh's parents sharing stories of his life and trying to ease the hurt we were all feeling. The local television and newspapers had not yet released his name. The coroner had held back, as the inquest into his death had not yet been opened and his body had not been released. We were told this was due to happen very soon and the police had advised us to write a statement to be released to the media. We all agreed that he was a private man, who had died in a public way, and that it was of no concern to anyone outside the family. We were advised that as soon as the inquest was opened it would be adjourned, to give the British Transport Police time to investigate what had happened. The police told us that if we released a statement, the family would be left alone. We were reliably informed that if we did not do this once Tosh's details were released we could have reporters at our doors, waiting for our side of the story.

This proved to be true and hours after Tosh's details were out I had three reporter's cards and one letter through the letterbox at the flat. I was later told by a neighbour that they knocked on her door for details of who Tosh was and asked her what she knew of his lifestyle. As we were new to the area she said she knew nothing, but she did tell me later even if she had known anything she would not have told them. That same neighbour admitted that she had learned of Tosh's death when she saw his photo on the television news. It was a shock, she said, to see her neighbour announced as dead on the news. She had recognised his face, although she did not know his name at the time.

A police press man came and took a brief statement which he read back to us. He asked if we had a photo in mind to be put out with the statement and we replied that we'd not thought that far ahead. He was quite a young man and I think a bit insensitive to the grief the family was suffering. Mentioning that he had tracked down a photo from Tosh's Norfolk County Council ID card, he proceeded to show us his find. With no warning, he held up a full A4 size photo of Tosh. I thought it was a good likeness, as I had seen him alive only a few days before. This was not the case for his family. They had not had time to adjust to their son and brother without hair, minus the beard and no longer wearing glasses. People's appearances can change dramatically in fifteen years. His parents broke down sobbing and his mum just collapsed. I think he could have left the photo on the table face down for us to look at in private, rather than causing the instant shock that rippled through the room. The picture was released and copies were given to us as the last picture of Tosh alive.

The press statement was passed out to the media through the police press office on our behalf and it appeared in print the following day, with an extra spin on Tosh's love of Poker and Gambling. He was a licenced bookmaker when we first met and a love of greyhounds, racehorses and casinos were the norm in our lives together. The piece in the paper made him out to be a gambler, but gamblers take many forms and he was not a gambler in the true sense of the word. In his lifetime he had played the stock market, worked at a racetrack and greyhound stadiums in Great Yarmouth and Swaffham. I learned to 'tic tac' and in our early days together I worked as his tic tac in the evening, still employed in my full time job during the day. He was a controlled gambler and his main love towards the end of his life was Poker. We had shared three wonderful trips to the 'City of Neon', Las Vegas. I am a great lover of Elvis Presley and live music; in most cities around the world, where there is a casino there is almost certainly a theatre or cinema nearby. Las Vegas is a city we both loved.

Whilst all this was going on, I was helping Vanessa gather information for the British Transport Police for their investigation. The British Transport Police wanted the service history of the car Tosh was driving, to check the car had not been faulty. The car had been serviced only a few weeks before and the MOT was good for another year. I also had to inform DVLA that the car was no longer on the road. They could not accept this information over the phone, but needed it in writing, so I typed the letter and saved it on my computer at home. After I had saved the letter, I went back to the document folder to check it was still there and I saw a file named 'Goodbye Lucy'. I called Val to come through. I had found the letter from Tosh, saying he could no longer cope with the worry he was causing me, or himself, that he would love me forever and not to hate him for what he was going to do. He also said this would give me a chance at a new life. I did not know what shift pattern Vanessa was on, but I felt this was a time to use the 24/7 number she had given me.

So, with shaking hands, I dialled the mobile number. Vanessa answered straight away, she was off duty walking the dog. I apologised for calling her, but I thought she should know what I had found. She asked me to print a couple of copies (I printed a few more to give to Tosh's family), then close the letter and she would seek further advice and come back to me. Again, she was her usual considerate self, asking how I felt, if I was alone and reassuring me that I was not to be concerned about calling her because that's what she was there for. I know this sounds strange, but I was relieved that I had found the letter. Up until this point I was amazed and confused that nothing had been found. Tosh was a planner and I was not comfortable that he had done this terrible thing on a whim. Vanessa had warned me not to consider suicide until the investigation was over and the inquest decided the cause of death. I was comforted that Tosh had been thinking of me and his words told me the love we shared had not been one-sided. However mixed up his mind had been, he had still known that I was there for him. That meant the world to me.

Vanessa called back later the next day, saying that she needed a statement from me for the investigation. The British Transport Police had been in contact with her and she had agreed to take a statement from me on their behalf. Norfolk Police were not involved in the investigation, but Vanessa said she would do this for them as she and I felt so comfortable together. She thought this would be easier than talking to another stranger. Again, she was right.

Vanessa came to Val's home to take my statement and it took about three hours to go from my first meeting Tosh to the day of his death. Vanessa let me ramble on, noting down the dates and places we had shared our lives. It felt very personal to tell someone I had known barely two weeks about my life with Tosh. Vanessa then left to type up the statement, agreeing to return later to take me back to the flat to look at the 'Goodbye Lucy' letter. The neighbours at Val's house had noted the police car thinking that Val's son, Glenn, was in trouble. They had no idea of the real reason the police car was at Val's house for so long.

Vanessa was still on duty, when she called back, still in full uniform with the brightly coloured car. When Val opened the door, Vanessa shouted 'Hello Val, is Lucy ready?' As I arrived at the door Val shouted across that I had been looking forward to a ride in a police car. 'If she's any trouble, Vanessa, you can always handcuff her!' Vanessa laughed and shouted back 'I better not, she might like it!' Again, Vanessa could sense this was going to be another emotional trip back to the flat that Tosh and I had shared and she tried to lighten the mood with her sense of humour. The time spent taking down my statement had made me think about everything Tosh and I had shared during our life together. My emotions were up and down constantly. I am not sure if Vanessa knew this at the time, but she had a wonderful way of judging the situation to make the official paperwork she needed from me easier to cope with. During the short time we had spent together she had gauged when I needed to laugh or cry, to release the strain on my emotions. She gave me a hug as I reached the car and she asked if I was ok. I told her I was.

When we got to the flat I opened the door and Vanessa trudged up the stairs. She got to the top of the stairs and stopped. 'Don't move, don't touch anything.' 'Why?' I replied. 'I think you've been burgled.' 'What have they taken?' I asked. Vanessa said they had only left the TV, the sofa, the bed and the computer with its desk. I laughed. Vanessa was joking. Tosh and I had moved nineteen times in our sixteen years together, so we never collected furniture or possessions. It was a practical thing and I could pack the whole house up in three to four hours. Having no furniture or personal items had not seemed unusual at the time, considering the life we had chosen to live.

We went into the kitchen, still laughing, and fired up the computer. The technical people at Police Headquarters had written Vanessa some instructions on how to 'look behind' the 'Goodbye Lucy', letter to see when it was created. He had typed it at around 10.15am on the Thursday prior to his death on the Sunday. We screen printed the information that was needed and another couple of copies of the letter too. Vanessa signed and dated them, to prove she had witnessed this information being extracted from my computer.

We were about to leave the flat, when I mentioned to Vanessa about her footwear. The first day she came to the flat she sat at my feet and she was wearing the regulation footwear (as she always is) and whatever she had stood in that day had transferred to my carpet. It was a rented flat, so I had to make sure the mark came out and it was difficult to clean off! So if a police officer comes into your home, make sure they wipe their feet!

We made our way back to the car and Vanessa produced the typed statement for me to read through and sign. I have had many varied experiences in my life, but until Tosh's death I had never been in a police car. It is a novel experience to see how most other drivers react when you pull out into traffic. I love people watching and this was just another way to indulge myself. Vanessa warned me that she was on duty and if she got a call she would not have time to drop me off and she would just have to go! As a traffic PC, her car was her office and the radio was on constantly when Vanessa was with me and, in between the bleeping, information was coming through about lots of incidents around the county. I was amazed that anything was understood as it seemed a jumble of sounds to me, but unfazed by anything Vanessa was able to listen to the radio, talk to me and drive the car whilst being aware of everything around us! I was struggling to read the statement as the light was fading, but Vanessa stretched to reach between the seats and a little spotlight appeared. It was used mainly for reading maps and other documents in the dark, but it served the purpose I needed it for.

As we drove back to Val's house, Vanessa was cursing a male driver in front of us. She warned me that he was driving like an idiot and of the need to follow him if she was concerned. In front of us was a speed camera and we had followed this driver through traffic lights and over a roundabout, but he had not noticed us. It must be hard to not spot such a visible car with a strip of blue light attached to the roof in your rear view mirror! Just before the speed camera, he slowed his speed and drove perfectly. I asked if he had seen us, but Vanessa said she was convinced it was just the speed camera that improved his driving technique, not the sight of us. This being the case, Vanessa was happy he was with it enough not to be pulled over and we got back to Val's without incident. I passed the statement back, covered in corrections and red pen. She said it was like being back at school. I had initialled the changes and Vanessa took the statement back to correct and retype. It had been typed in a hurry, so I forgave her.

# CHAPTER EIGHT

Once Tosh's body had been released, the next major decision was regarding funeral arrangements. Tosh's parents wanted to make the arrangements and I agreed on certain conditions - number one being that in Tosh's Will he had specified that he wanted to be cremated, and number two that I would pay for the funeral from his estate. Marlene and Bramwell (Tosh's parents) went off to the local funeral director to begin the planning process. The family was gathered to discuss the arrangements. Tosh was not a religious man, so it was arranged for the service to be taken by a lay person. The gentleman came and had a chat with us, to plan what we would like him to say. None of us felt emotionally strong enough that we could stand up and speak about Tosh, so the man listened to us talk about Tosh, his life and the things that had influenced him. It was agreed to play 'Memories' as we entered the crematorium. The Lord's Prayer was to be read and the well-known words 'Don't stand at my grave and weep' seemed appropriate. We needed two further songs to be played in between the words and this was the hardest part of the planning, because Tosh had been apart from his family and had taken his own life, most of the traditional songs were not suitable.

As I mentioned, I am a huge Elvis Presley fan and Marlene and Bramwell thought of 'Always On My mind'. Another suggestion was 'A Deck of Cards' to touch on the gambling theme. However, once listened carefully to the song it became clear that it was about a soldier returning from war, remembering his friends who had died. Bramwell thought of 'My Way'. It is a lovely song, either by Elvis or Frank Sinatra, but when I mentioned it could be thought of in two ways - one being that he lived his life his way (that was obviously what Bramwell was thinking) which was fine, but some may believe we were thinking of his death and him doing that his way. Not really right for this occasion. We all said we would think overnight and discuss any ideas the next day. Trying to avoid songs with mentions of family and loved ones, or trains or cars, was difficult.

I arrived back at Val's and chatted to her son, Glenn, about this.

Glenn's musical taste included some songs from the Seventies and he could think of lots of music I had never even heard of. My musical taste is largely 1950s and 1960s, including Elvis, Cliff Richard, The Everly Brothers, Connie Francis and Del Shannon. I also love Kenny Rogers, Garth Brooks and various American Country artists. Most of my musical taste included what Tosh hated. He was not a great one for music, but he did like Neil Young and when we were first together he played Neil Young's 'After the Gold Rush', along with Tracy Chapman cassettes in the car and in the flat. Another artist he liked in our early days together was Eric Clapton and 'Wonderful Tonight' was a romantic song that we loved listening to together.

Eventually he moved on to Morrissey and The Smiths, not a musical taste I shared. The Smiths seemed to me to sing such depressive songs and their lyrics seemed to have no meaning in my ears. Who knows, maybe there was some kind of connection here and Tosh had endured low moments further back than even he could have recalled.

Glenn and I spent the evening going through the old cassettes from a shoe box, found at the bottom of the wardrobe in his old room, and after lots of suggestions- some serious and some unprintable- he suggested 'Forever Autumn' by Justin Hayward of the Moody Blues. It was fitting to think of life being cold and turning to Winter without him around. I got a copy from the library to play to the others. We had to listen to it a couple of times, because we were crying, but it was agreed we had one of the songs we needed. I have a DVD of Tosh playing Live Poker in the Northern Ireland Open in Belfast; in the background they were playing 'The Gambler' by Kenny Rogers. This song tells the story of a gambler playing his last Poker game and passing his wisdom onto another gambler. I listened to the words and played it for the family. They all agreed and it was another box ticked.

As Tosh was to be cremated, we had decided on a cardboard coffin. There would be family flowers only and donations to the two charities named in our Wills, The Injured Jockeys Fund and Cancer Research. The family flowers were a large horseshoe covered with gold flowers, with red flowers placed where the nails would have been to nail the shoe to the hoof. The horseshoe was for two reasons. Firstly, to represent horseracing and the part it had played in Tosh's life. Secondly, a horseshoe is known for good luck, to gamblers (and others) worldwide. The colour gold was for the riches he had experienced in his life and any winnings are known to be golden. The coffin could be any colour, so we chose green to represent the turf of the racecourse. I had one concern and, as I felt more comfortable with Marlene and Bramwell, I knew I could ask the question burning in my head.

'What if it rains?' Everyone looked at me as if to say what does she mean? I wondered, if the coffin was cardboard what happens if it gets wet? Marlene began to laugh, 'Lucy, you are priceless!' I went on, 'if the cardboard gets wet, how will he not fall out?' I was told the cardboard was treated against wetness. I had visions of a cardboard box getting wet and collapsing into a soggy mess. The laughter did ease the tension in the room and everyone relaxed again. We had passed another difficult milestone in planning the funeral. Considering I was a stranger, my thoughts and opinions were listened to carefully. Again, I am amazed at the acceptance of me as part of this close family, at such a traumatic time in their lives. I had never even been to a funeral before and, at the age of thirty seven years old, I was planning the funeral of my life partner. There are certain times in life when we are left to flounder. No set rules or guidance are given on how to react to a death, or a sudden death in this case. We were all finding our own ways of coping.

# CHAPTER NINE

Tosh was an incredible planner. Everything had to be in order and neat and tidy. I was the opposite. Early on in our relationship, it was decided that he would do the paperwork and financial stuff like settling the bills. He had been a self-employed person, both as a qualified electrician and as a licensed bookmaker. Both jobs needed paperwork completed for financial reasons, as well as keeping up with legal regulations. He ran our finances as he had run his businesses. Everything was together in an envelope. The paperwork for the car was in an envelope marked 'Car', the paperwork for the rental agreement on the flat we were living in was in an envelope marked 'Flat Rental', the pension details were in an envelope marked 'Pensions'. You can get the picture. He also had a folder containing bills and official papers. These were in date order and when a bill was paid, details of when, how and how much was noted on the bill, with receipts where they were available. If he queried or questioned anything, details were written on the bill too. The date, time and who he spoke to were noted. This was one of his good habits and one I have taken on board myself. It made life so much easier when I began to sort out the paperwork.

I was sorting out the essential paperwork that needs to be processed when someone dies. Tosh's life insurance and car insurance were both with the same company. I began by calling the car insurance number first, to notify them that the car was off the road. When I explained why the car was off the road and what had happened, I was put on hold whilst the man spoke to his supervisor. Vanessa had warned me that the train company may want to claim back the money for the train and the damage to the train. The man came back on the phone and explained he needed to take down some details. He took down the details of the policy, of Tosh, of where the car was now and who was investigating the accident. He asked if the car could be viewed by the insurance company and I explained to him that the car burst into flames on the impact of the train, but the recovery company the police had used could advise him of the details and gave their number and address. He explained that there was legal cover with the policy if I needed a solicitor and took my contact number and promised to be in touch soon.

He was more nervous than me and kept telling me how calm I was. He then tried to transfer me to the life insurance department. The company played the music of Frank Sinatra whilst you are put on hold. I love Frank most of the time, but the loop of music had moved onto 'I get a kick out of you', which was not the most appropriate tune when I was phoning to tell them my partner had died. I didn't think the life insurance policy would pay out, as suicide had been mentioned, but I wanted to cease paying the premiums. When the phone was answered again, more details were taken and I was asked to send a death certificate. I explained that because of the inquest I would not get a death certificate until the investigation was complete, which could be many months. I did have a temporary one from the coroner and was told this would be fine. He said usually he would need the original to be able to release the funds, but under the circumstances the temporary one would be fine. I asked if they had to wait for the outcome of the inquest, in case his death was caused by suicide. He replied that it made no difference, as the policy paid out on suicide provided the claim was not made in the first twelve months and this policy had been running for over five years. I put the phone down in a daze and tried to explain to Val what he had said, when I was interrupted by my mobile. It was the car insurance man. He said he had not said anything earlier, as he had to speak to his manager (he was in a call centre in Glasgow), but he wanted to send me some flowers. I said that was not necessary, but he insisted that he wanted to because this was the first death he had had to deal with and I had sounded so calm on the phone, it had really helped him and he wanted to thank me. I gave him Val's address and then put the phone down and burst into tears. I could cope with the details and explaining what had happened, these were just facts that needed to be told, but the moment someone was nice or kind to me I just went to pieces.

I don't know what I would have done without the hugs and tissues from Val! When we got back to Val's house we struggled to get in the door, as there was a huge basket of flowers in the way. These were delivered earlier from my work colleagues. I knew I had a couple of people I would call friends but these flowers were too much. What is it that makes people so kind at times like this? Also delivered that day was a brown envelope, containing cards and messages from the people in my office. I was overcome. I did not know people even knew who I was, but here were messages and cards that told me different. I was overwhelmed and cried buckets at people's kind words and thoughtful phrases.

The next day, another flower arrangement arrived, from the insurance company. It meant so much that someone in Glasgow was sending me flowers, because he thought I was coping and being so brave. He would be requesting them back if he saw me, as I was not being that brave when I looked at them. The tears and emotions flowed again.

With my emotions being so up and down, I began to appreciate the love and hugs I had been given. Tosh was not a touchy, feely person and we had different ideas on sharing emotions; it took him many years before he told me that he loved me. Until then he had just said he had affection for me! I am a tactile person, who loves to be hugged and hug back, but Tosh would never sit on the sofa and hold hands whilst watching television. We did not share the same taste in films, so we never got to sit on the back row in the cinema together.

Tosh was very reserved and of the opinion that love and emotions were not shared in public. In the privacy of our bedroom, he was more caring and romantic, but this did not often extend to the other side of that door. He would walk along the street hand-in-hand, but that would be as far as he went. I am sure he had lots of emotions within, but had no idea how to express them. It was as though he did not want to show a chink in his armour to make him appear weak. I did not realise how much I missed the value of a hug or being loved without any barriers, until I was hugged and loved without caution again by both families and friends.

We always knew that we loved each other. I never doubted he loved me and I am sure he knew I loved him too, but he did not show it in an open and public way. I will never know if this was his way, or just a part of coping with the depression, not allowing his emotions to reach the surface and not permitting others to share their emotions with him.

# CHAPTER TEN

The day of the funeral arrived and Tosh's family were due to follow the hearse in a funeral car from Marlene and Bramwell's home. As I was uncertain of my emotions and did not want to intrude on their private family time, I opted to meet them there. My friend Val agreed to be with me throughout. As her husband David was a friend of Tosh's he also came with us. The day was a cold November day and when we arrived at the crematorium we were ushered into the waiting room. When I got there, the room was crowded and I was overwhelmed by the sea of faces all looking in my direction.

Mum and Dad came over and gave me a huge hug. My twin came over and did the same. Her husband was also there, as he had been friends with Tosh long before I had met him. My younger sister Katherine was at home, as she had just been released from hospital after having her wisdom teeth removed. Her husband, Peter, was at home to keep an eye on her as the anaesthetic meant someone had to watch her for twenty four hours.

I looked at the sea of faces and recognised some of Tosh's old friends, some of whom I was told had been at school with him. His aunts and uncles came and introduced themselves to me once they realised who I was. The names and faces were all a blur. Then the hearse arrived and I stood and watched as the pallbearers removed the coffin. More hugs were exchanged with his family, before we followed the coffin inside. Everyone was wearing bright colours as we had requested, so it was good to see our wishes had been considered – we thought the day would be hard enough without black ties and suits.

The pallbearers told me later they felt very strange not wearing suits and that it even felt disrespectful. They were in jeans and casual jackets and the layman who was leading the service admitted he had bought a new shirt and tie, as his wardrobe was full of white shirts and black ties. Today he was wearing a lilac shirt with a lilac and purple tie.

The service was a brief affair. The words spoken about Tosh made it sound like the man had met him, which was wonderful. Tosh's picture sat on top of the coffin and as the curtains closed on his life Kenny Rogers sang 'The Gambler'. Most people were tapping their feet to the song, which was what we wanted. The service should reach its conclusion on a happy note, not a sad one.

The family were led out to the Garden of Remembrance to read the notes on the flowers and meet the people who had attended the funeral. When I got outside, I paused to greet Tosh's old friends and members of his family.

Tosh and I had lived our lives as a lone couple for so long I had no idea anyone would register the fact that he had died. It affected me and his family because we had lost someone we loved and would never see again. However, I was overwhelmed by the support from others who had turned up for his funeral that day.

I was surprised to see so many employees of Norfolk County Council. I had been employed by them since we returned from Spain in October 2001 and tended to keep myself to myself. I did not feel comfortable socialising outside work. I had a life with Tosh and work was work, so I did not know that so many people would be moved enough to attend Tosh's funeral in order to support me. Some Senior Managers from Education Personnel, as well as my new team in HR were in attendance. I felt quite ashamed I had not noticed them before and just got on with my life, not even realising they knew my name.

So many friends from my office had turned out and many of them were crying or close to tears. This was the first time I had seen anyone from the office and they were amazed how calm and controlled I was. I think this was because it was only two weeks since Tosh's death and so much had happened I had not really had any time for me. There had been so much to sort out, from meeting both families again, sorting out the paperwork Vanessa needed, contacting insurance companies and DVLA, as well as planning the funeral.

The time between a death and the funeral is like a runaway train, with decisions that have to be made that could not be put off. Tosh had worked on and off for various departments at Norfolk County Council, but one of the jobs he enjoyed most there was as a Trading Standards Officer. As I continued through the gardens, I was greeted by Tosh's old colleagues from Norfolk County Council Trading Standards. Many of them are still in contact with me to this day.

Also in attendance were some of his old drinking buddies from our early years. Many of them had known Tosh since High School. It brought back many memories of our early time together, after hours drinking, steak sandwiches, pool and Thin Lizzy on the jukebox.

I was surprised that so many people had made the effort to attend and some were there to purely show support for me. However, considering we had spent nearly sixteen years with just the two of us, I was happily surprised to see so many faces. It just shows how many people Tosh had been in contact with over the years and how he was thought of by their presence there on that day. It's funny how we go through life thinking we were not being noticed and the main time people show they knew you, or cared for you, is the time when you are no longer there. Like at your funeral.

Just as I got to the flowers, the weather had turned very cold and the snow started to fall. The flowers were collected by the funeral director, to be taken on to the internment due to take place on Monday. Tosh's parents wanted his ashes buried so they had somewhere to go and spend quiet times and remember their son. Tosh's wishes were to be cremated. What happened to him after this was out of his control, of course, but I think he would have liked to have been scattered in the casinos in Las Vegas, but this was no longer a practical solution for his reunited family. It wouldn't exactly be easy to jet over to Las Vegas when we wanted to feel close to him, so permission was granted for him to be interned with his grandparents in Ashwellthorpe.

After the funeral, Marlene and Bramwell had invited their children and grandchildren back to their home to have something to eat and remember Tosh. I was included and took Val with me. We spent many hours chatting about Tosh and his life with his family and his life with me. Marlene brought out the family photograph album and it was lovely to share stories of happier times.

The next day, I went to the local florist to buy a single red rose. Two days later, Tosh's ashes were due to interned and the family flowers were going to be taken to the graveside by the funeral director, but I wanted a single flower to place as I said my final goodbye.

## CHAPTER ELEVEN

The Monday morning arrived and Val accompanied me to the graveyard. What would I have done without a friend like Val? How do you begin to repay such kindness and friendship? This was going to be an emotional day for Marlene and Bramwell too, as they were burying their son. I felt quite detached though, as I did not have any feelings of Tosh being present in any form. His ashes were in a little basket, a mini basket in the shape of an urn. The funeral director was there and so was Tosh's sister, Sue. Tosh's family each held the basket for a final hug, before a few words were said and Bramwell placed it in the ground. We all put some soil on top and I placed my rose as I said my goodbye. We all hugged again, before going our separate ways. It was a very quick service and our joint official duties had been completed.

I had a couple more days with Val, before planning to move back to my flat to start my new life. I had been off work for three weeks and compassionate leave would cover some of that time, but I would need a sick certificate from the doctor to cover the rest. The doctor I saw was the same doctor Tosh had seen, only a few weeks prior to his death. She had ignored his request for counselling, content to give him antidepressants which he never took. The prescription was found after his death. The doctor greeted me and offered her condolences. She asked how I was feeling and what could she do for me. Did I want bereavement counselling? No, I replied, I just wanted a certificate to return to work. She asked when I was planning to go back to work and I told her the next Monday, which was six days away. She asked what job I did and continued to ask if I wanted more time off.

Under the circumstances, I could take as much time off work as I wanted, but I pointed out that it would serve no purpose to remain off work. I had only taken three weeks off because there had been a delay in Tosh's body being released for the funeral. The doctor wrote out the certificate and asked if I wanted any sleeping tablets or antidepressants. I told her she would be wasting her paper, as I would not be taking anything.

I think I was still furious with her for not offering Tosh counselling when he asked for help, instead of prescribing tablets that he explained he did not want. She was still really keen to offer the tablets to me.... I wonder if she's on commission?!

I think from my experience with doctors over the years they don't seem to have much time for people anymore. Is it because we all move around too much and they don't get to know their patients? Do they just want us out as quickly as possible, to tick another box on their performance targets and quotas?

When Tosh had approached his doctor for help a few weeks before his death he was not a time waster, but genuinely wanting some assistance and reassurance. At first he was told I was not allowed to be present, due to patient and doctor confidentiality, but he persuaded the doctor to allow me to stay as he thought I might be able to explain things he might have missed in his upset state of mind. She brushed his questions of counselling aside and gave him a prescription for anti-depressants and some copies of notes about depression and panic attacks she had printed from internet websites.

It was hardly surprising that I had no patience with the same doctor about two months later, when Tosh had only been dead two and a half weeks.

I left the doctors' surgery with a certificate to allow me to return to work and the next day I returned to my flat. I moved the furniture around in the lounge and the bedroom and did a thorough spring clean too. I changed the duvet and pillows to the new ones that Tosh had bought the day before he died. I then removed all his toiletries from the bathroom and packed his clothes and shoes in a bag to be taken to the charity shop. I had kept back a couple of polo shirts that I could use as he had only bought them a few weeks before. I also saved a cap he had worn in Las Vegas, to give to Marlene and Bramwell at a later date. It was quite late by the time I had completed my sorting out. It just seemed the logical thing to do at the time. His clothes were not going to be worn by him again and I had no thoughts of having his things around. I have since met people who have wardrobes full of clothes two years after their husband or wife has died. I know we are all different, but I did not see the point and it served no purpose on the comfort scale. It just reminded me that he was not around to wear the clothes any longer. There is not a right or wrong time, no set rule, just how it feels for the person left behind.

Some people are comforted by sleeping under a duvet that smells of their husband or wife. I have met widows and widowers who buy perfume or aftershave to keep a familiar smell around them. It is also not unusual to keep clothes to hug and smell whilst grieving alone. It just goes to show that the experience and process of grieving is different for everybody.

I signed onto my computer account to check my emails and I noticed that my twin was signed in online. I started chatting to her and realised after a short while I was in fact chatting to her husband. The username they jointly use to sign online with does not tell you who is typing back the messages, so it can cause confusion! Many people have asked me how I coped on the first night back in the flat alone and I can honestly say I was not alone, as I was chatting online with my brother-in-law until around one or two o'clock in the morning. He had known Tosh long before I did and we shared our memories of him. I had many caring online chats with him over the next few weeks. He helped me over some very tearful and lonely nights. For this kindness I will always be grateful.

The next few days were spent notifying official people and organisations of Tosh's death and getting the utilities and council tax in my own name, informing them I was a single occupant. I also had to look at the finances in detail. I had yet to pay for the funeral and keep on top of the bills, so many outstanding and final payments needed to be paid at this time and it felt like all my money was slipping away fast. I needed to know that I had enough money coming in to cover the outgoings. Working out my budget, I soon discovered I was not covering my outgoings with only one income. I still had to buy a car, as Tosh kindly took his journey onto the railway line in our only vehicle. My brother-in-law found a car for me, but I could not pick it up until after Christmas and that was still three weeks away.

I returned to work and a ten minute car journey now meant two buses and an additional hour on my journey each way - and that was if the buses ran to time. When I got to work, I was greeted by a sea of faces and lots of questions. Some people were worried about me and others were curious about what Tosh had done. I had coped really well and I think I shocked lots of people with my attitude to my newly bereaved status. I think I let the side down, because I was not dressed in black, or wearing a headscarf, and crying out 'woe is me'. With those people who asked about Tosh, I came out with the standard reply that he was train spotting without his glasses, so he had to get close to read the train's number. I don't think this gallows humour went down too well, but the people who were given this response did not really care about me they just wanted the latest gossip and a possible suicide must have been an extremely juicy titbit for them.

Being a bereaved person, whatever your age, scares other people. At the age of thirty seven, I had not met many bereaved people and here I was finding myself in that exact situation. It's like it must have felt to be a leper. People will talk about you behind your back and the room will fall silent as you enter it. People will feel uncomfortable and not know the right thing to say to you, so they either avoid you, or bringing up the subject of death, or tell you 'you will soon be over it', or 'as you are so young you will soon meet someone new.' No-one has told me to 'pull yourself together', but I have spoken to other widows who have been told this by 'well-meaning' friends and relatives. You can imagine the mouthful people would have got from me, had they offered this helpful platitude to me!

Those who really were concerned were also not given the real me. Val and Vanessa had been the closest to seeing the real me, warts and all. I certainly didn't wish to show the real me to outsiders. It was not a conscious thought, it's not like I decided what to say to people, or choose who would see my emotions, it was just what happened. I simply answered the questions and queries as honestly as I could when they came up. A bit too honestly some would say! If I came close to breaking down, it was with Val or Vanessa. For me it was a case of these were the facts, this had happened, I couldn't turn back time and return life back to how it was. I just had to adjust to each day as it came along, with all the new trials and tribulations that came with that. If people asked how I was feeling, I told them fine or as well as could be expected. What purpose would it serve to tell them the truth? Nine times out of ten when people ask how you are doing, they don't really want you to tell them truthfully. If you told them how you truly felt, you would scare them witless! They want you to say you are fine, because it makes them feel better. So 'I'm fine thanks' was an easy and automatic response.

One thing that did surprise me was that was that I could act my way out of my feelings. Everyone saw a girl of thirty seven coping after her partner had died. They did not see me crying myself to sleep, because I was scared to be alone and not having anyone to hug me and hold me. They did not see the worry when I could not pay my bills or make ends meet. To the public I was wonderful and brave and an inspiration. It was just a front! When I was alone, I was a mess! I was lonely, exhausted, but not able to sleep, worried and guilty and confused. Why had this happened to me? Why was my love for Tosh not enough to save him? Did he sense my patience, along with frustration at not really understanding his low moods, running out? Why did he not stay to work through it? We had been through so much, so why did he give up now? I was thirty seven and my life had been turned upside down and my heart inside out. I had never been to a funeral before in my life, his was my first, only adding to the trauma. The support I had been given up until the funeral was amazing and then people start to drift away. Their lives may have been touched by his death, but when they got home their lives were more or less the same. Mine will never be the same again.

Depression and mental illness is a very scary thing for the loved ones. We can only be there for them, loving them and worrying about them. I can't imagine how tormented someone must be to want to stop living. Logic does not appear in their thoughts. Lifting someone you love from the darkest moments is such a relief, but there are only so many times you can lift the mood, before they withdraw to the darkness of their minds and their worrying thoughts again. I know I had something many people will never have. I was loved by Tosh until he died, the note he left told me that. Knowing I was loved to the end helped me through the pain of losing him.

I felt so alone, yet overwhelmed by family too. For almost sixteen years I had no-one but Tosh and Val to worry about me. I was still having panic attacks at being surrounded by people. My past life meant that I had lost the social skills needed to hold a conversation and this panic and worry included both families. It is not something you can relearn overnight, it takes time. Now I was not alone but had Mum, Dad, Marlene, Bramwell, Val, Vanessa and Kath and Peter (my younger sister and her husband). There are many others, but it would take too long to list them all. Sometimes I would get home tired and weary, just wanting to have some peace and work out how to make a meal. Tosh had been a househusband, he had cooked, cleaned, shopped, laundered and ironed all our clothes, maintained a smooth running house and car, paid the bills. I just went to work and it worked very well for us. Now my stability was gone and I was on the steepest learning curve of my life. I had to learn everything again, but instantly, not gradually. I needed to eat and have clean clothes.

When I got home from work I would make the simplest of meals, just sit down to eat, and the phone would ring. I know people were worried and cared about me, but what they did not understand was that if they all called it meant I had a whole evening of 'Hello, how are you today?' calls. It was exhausting. It also meant I was eating a lot of cold meals, as the phone always rang when I was about to eat. My solution was an answerphone. They could leave a message and I could call them back. Vanessa was not a problem, as her shift pattern meant she generally called later in the evening. Also, I was not trying to fill in missing years with Vanessa, so if I was having a sad day or had dealt with a bit of official paperwork that had got to me I could be open and when she asked 'How are you doing?' I could respond honestly. If I had told the truth to the others it would have worried them and what would be gained by that? I was trying to shield them from more hurt and pain. I did feel I was juggling this strange life, two reunited families, work, buses and feeding myself.

Who could I speak to, except Vanessa? None of them had been bereaved at the age of thirty seven, by suspected suicide, and all the prejudices that go with it. Mum and Dad were just relieved to have their daughter back. Marlene and Bramwell had just lost their son and were grieving for him, Val had her own family. Kath was wonderful, but I was only just getting to know her as an adult, she was still at school when I left the family all that time ago so I did not know her well enough to share all my worries. I did not want to frighten her by letting her know her big sister was not coping. It felt as if everyone wanted a piece of me and had expectations of me; I felt I could not deliver.

Coping with grief is an exhausting business. I have since discovered a whole network of widows supporting each other, so they don't have to frighten family and friends, but I did not find them until fourteen months after Tosh died - too late for me during the toughest period - so I just coped alone.

When you begin to pick up the pieces of 'normal' life, that's when you need the support of family and friends, but they have gone back to their own lives and, as they see from the external front that it seems you are coping, they assume you are fine. That's often far from the truth. How could you be fine already after such a dramatic loss?

## CHAPTER TWELVE

Then, suddenly and out of the blue I was given a Christmas card, which had been sent to my Mum's address. Mum gave it to me and told me there had been others over the years but this was the first year she could pass it on, as she had not known where I was in previous years.

The card was from an old friend. Edward had been my friend since I was about thirteen years old, when we were in youth club together. We became good friends when I went to London to work as a nanny and he was training to be a nurse. The business card enclosed in the Christmas card told me that he was now ordained and working as a Chaplain in the RAF. The last time we had been in contact had been on his wedding day. I had put his buttonhole on for him, wished him lots of happiness, and stood back and watched him marry another girl. We had been close friends in the past, however, friendship was as far as we had gone, so it was not strange for anyone to see me invited to watch him marry someone else. Our paths did not cross after this and I went off to my exciting life with Tosh and put Edward on the memory shelf of my mind. That is where he stayed for about eighteen years.

The Christmas card had details of the airbase where he was currently stationed. I had been bereaved only a month when I got this card and, seeing the address where he was based, I assumed he had sent it because he had seen the news and read the local papers. So, I wrote off a long letter thanking him for his support and explained about Tosh's death and hoped he and his family were happy and healthy. I had written many letters of thanks in the last month and had no reason to believe this one was any different. I posted it and got on with my life.

Just two days later I was cleaning the flat. The buses had been late and the meal I had cooked was barely edible, so my mood was quite low and I was feeling sad and sorry for myself. The telephone rang and I cursed it, thinking that another caller was checking on me. This was a terrible thought to have had, because they were only calling to show they cared about me. However, I did not want to ignore it and worry the caller, in case they thought there was something to be concerned about. So I answered the phone. This was my lifeline. It was Edward. The friendship we had shared in the past, made it seem like we had only had a break of a few days, not almost eighteen years. We talked for around two hours. He admitted he had not heard the news of Tosh's death, but he had been sending Christmas cards every year to my Mum's because he did not have a forwarding address.

We talked about his family and his life in the RAF. I talked about my life with Tosh and what had happened leading up to his death. I was fine just telling facts and details, he then made the fateful error of asking me how I was coping. I just burst into tears. I apologised and told him I was fine and not to worry. He replied 'Lucy how could you be fine with all that has happened?' Continuing, he pointed out that it was not problem to cry, it was a human reaction. I seemed to be more tearful when people were nice to me. That is when my emotional barrier crumbles. Although he had not been bereaved himself, he let me relax and voice thoughts I could not tell family members. During that first two hours conversation we connected again. I could be me again, just like I could with Vanessa. We promised to stay in touch and if we needed to talk we agreed to call each other. Mobile numbers and email addresses were exchanged and I wished him and his family a healthy and happy Christmas. It was 22nd December after all.

When the first Christmas of my new life arrived, I had been alone for just over a month. Mum and Dad wanted me to spend it with them; Marlene and Bramwell wanted me to stay with them; my friends in Ireland, who Tosh and I had met when we all lived in Spain, wanted me to go and have a break with them. I simply wanted some time to myself. I was still without a car, so I decided to have Christmas Day alone. With no bus service on Christmas Day or Boxing Day, I was a sitting duck. Unless I was taken somewhere they all knew I would be at home. Telling everyone that I wanted my first Christmas alone, I had it all planned. I was going to sleep in, then have a large pot of tea and hot buttered toast and laze about in my play clothes. I did not have to get dressed up and planned to eat chocolates, drink red wine and watch black and white films on the television. My Christmas lunch was going to be steak, onion rings and potato wedges, followed by Smarties ice cream. Everyone knew of my plans. They thought I was mad, but said it was my choice. I had been brought up as a Christian but felt I was not worthy enough to return to the church yet, because Tosh and I had never married and due to the way he ended his life. I knew the one time people went to church was either Christmas or Easter and I did not want to be a once a year church goer...when I was ready to return it would be my decision.

My Christmas Day was stretching before me. A day I did not need to be anywhere or be polite to anyone. A day for ME!! This lasted until ten thirty, when Tosh's sister and her partner Roger arrived with chocolates and presents from themselves and Marlene and Bramwell. I was still not used to entertaining or holding conversations, but I was polite and my "Equity card" came into it's own as I entertained my newly acquired sister-in-law and her partner, who claimed they were just passing. I think this was unlikely, as they had the presents and chocolates with them. They left around two thirty in the afternoon and the rest of the day was my own. Boxing Day I had to myself. Then Val picked me up the next day and I spent a happy family day with her family. I have so much to be thankful for, my life could have been so different.

Between Christmas and New Year I picked up my car. I had also been lucky enough to have some money come in via a life insurance policy and Tosh's County Council pension. As we were not married, the pension came in the form of a death in service grant, which was to be a one-off payment. This helped at the time and enabled me to buy the second hand car. I also decided the time was right to buy some furniture, so I bought a coffee table and a shelf unit. This may not be big news to most people, but my furniture until this point was a bed, sofa, television, computer, desk and chair, cooker, washing machine and a fridge. Not much to show for sixteen years of life with Tosh. During this time I could pride myself on being able to pack up the whole house in four hours! This had been done on a few occasions. So it was exciting to be buying my new coffee table and shelf unit. I was trying to be independent, so planned to collect the furniture, which was flat pack, in my new little car. I mentioned it in passing to Mum and Dad, in my excitement, and my solo adventure was taken over by them. They arrived at the flat at nine in the morning, claiming that I would never fit the furniture into my car without help. So off we went to collect it. We loaded up Mum and Dad's car and took it all back to the flat. I was so excited, but wanted to show my independence by building it myself. So my first New Year's Eve was spent building my new furniture. I am now queen of the allan key. In the instructions it is best to ignore the words 'simple and easy to assemble'. This is complete rubbish! The instructions and pictures are written and taken by technical experts who have built these things before. The shelf unit was assembled and in the instructions it said to tighten all the screws and bolts. When I found I had missed one, the whole thing had to come apart and I had to begin again.

My plan was to assemble the furniture and have a roast dinner to celebrate, with a couple of glasses of wine to see the New Year in. I did do all of these things, but my roast dinner was eaten surrounded by boxes, paper and parts of my new furniture. By one thirty in the morning I had achieved my goal. On completing such achievements I am so excited, I just want to share them with someone. This was when I felt so alone again, unable to talk to someone close to me about the experience there and then. I really did feel like I was going mad at times, I would find myself telling Tosh of my achievements. Of course, I realised he was not around, but it still felt like he would have been proud of what I had done. I was proud of what I had done.

From speaking to many bereaved people, following my own bereavement,

I was warned that some of the worst days to live through would be birthdays, Christmas and New Year.

I have to admit I did not feel the same way, due to the way I had lived my life over the previous decade and a half. During my time with Tosh, we had chosen not to celebrate birthdays and Christmas. It started out as a financial decision, as money was really tight in the early days and our birthdays always seemed to coincide with some disaster that had struck us.

We did not have material things, there seemed little point at the time in buying things for each other, things that we didn't need or would not use. Moving house so many times makes you think twice before buying clutter that only takes up space. If we did buy something for each other it would often be something boring, but practical, like a new coat or boots.

Since Tosh's death, my New Year seems to begin from the thirteenth of November not the first of January, like most people. I am assuming this will gradually move back in line with the rest of the world, but when my life changed in November 2005 it seemed to be the date when I started my life again. I can always look back at how far I have progressed from that date onwards.

My birthdays have been shared with my family since my life totally altered. Kath and Pete have included me in their lives and their circle of friends. Kath, Pete and Kath's friend Dan have all been welcomed to my home and I have cooked and enjoyed their friendship and love. I have come to realise that I enjoy buying presents and cards for others, but still struggle with the concept of them buying for me. It feels a bit uncomfortable and I believe sometimes that I don't deserve to be given such gifts. On reflection, I'm sure this is all linked to the newness of being shown love and kindness and it's something I need to adjust to in time.

I still have a panic attack when I am entertaining, whether it is Kath, Pete and Dan, or Mum and Dad, but hopefully this will improve in time as my confidence builds.

# CHAPTER THIRTEEN

As the New Year began I continued to fight with officialdom. Many problems I encountered were because we had different surnames. As Tosh had taken care of all the paperwork, lots of things were in his name. Jointly named things were fine i.e. utilities and bank accounts. My biggest problem was the phone line and internet connection, as I was living in a small village and the phone connection was the lifeline that kept me in contact with everyone. When I called to explain that Tosh had died they were perfectly fine in the way they responded. They would not close down the line, but give me twenty eight days to sort out the paperwork etc. to transfer the line into my name, notes were made on the file and for me to contact again when I was feeling strong enough to deal with the nitty gritty of forms. In the meantime, the joint bank account reverted to a single name. Unfortunately, this triggered a letter to be sent to Tosh from the phone company, asking him to contact them regarding his change in bank details.

I called them to explain and spoke to a man who was in a call centre in India. He had not read the note on his screen and could not understand why Tosh could not telephone himself! I was informed that no information could be changed on the account, without permission from Tosh. Eventually, I spoke to a supervisor, who said they needed a copy of the death certificate to make the necessary changes. Again, this was not possible because they did not recognise the temporary death certificate I had, pending the inquest. A full death certificate would not be available until the inquest had been completed and I had no details on when this would be. I was told that without a full death certificate and without Tosh's permission the telephone line was to be cut off, as the contract between the company and Tosh had been broken. I was told it would be seven days before it could be reconnected in my name and a new customer connection fee would be charged, as I was not one of their existing customers.

Frustration, anger and grief came over me and I burst into sobs of tears. This seemed to jolt them a bit and they waived the charges for the phone line, but not the internet connection. So, in the next thirty six hours, my phone line was cut off and I was without my lifeline for five days before they reconnected me free of charge. Needless to say, my internet connection was transferred to another company, but that's another story. I realise these are just everyday normal things to most people, but dealing with them alone when you are newly bereaved is emotional and unsettling. Goodness knows how hard it is to cope with all this for those who have children to look after and keep safe too. I only had me to look after!

On one of my emotionally stronger days, I answered the telephone and the company calling was trying to sell me a new fitted kitchen. They said they had called earlier and spoken to my husband, who had told them to call back and speak to the lady of the house to discuss it. I replied 'That's fine, but my husband died three months ago when a train hit his car. If you speak to him again can you ask him to call me as I have a few unanswered questions to put to him?' The line went deathly quiet and a mumbled apology was given and then the line went dead. Call centres put their staff under massive pressures to reach tough targets and I know they have a hard job to sell us stuff we don't really need. I know what it's like to need a sale to get paid. When we lived in Spain, I had a spell at selling timeshare over the phone. I was terrible and I only just sold enough to get paid each week. However, going back to this call, I know it was a bit mean of me to shock the kitchen salesman, but on that occasion I just couldn't help myself.

Early in the New Year, the funeral director sent Marlene and Bramwell the cards and letters that were sent with the floral donations. It was a Friday night, the weather was miserable and I had had a bad day at work. I came home to a dark, quiet and lonely flat. I turned on the radio for some noise and even that had moved off the station. I switched on the computer and had an inbox full of emails. I think there were about twelve or thirteen from Marlene. I had been feeling reality setting in that I was alone and Tosh was no longer here. Doing some soul searching about what I could have done to help him, I had come to the decision that I had done all that was possible at the time and it only resulted in me feeling even more lonely that my love was not enough for him to stay. I was feeling very low, but as usual I didn't want to worry anyone. Even Val, Vanessa and Edward were not privy to my feelings. I had to deal with this myself.

Seeing so many emails from Marlene just finished me off. Nine of the emails were scanned copies of the letters from those who had donated to the two charities instead of funeral flowers. Marlene had scanned them and emailed them to me. Unfortunately I could not read them once they were printed off. I was deeply upset by this and began to sob. The letters had been sent to Marlene and Bramwell, despite me writing to the funeral director when I settled the bill, requesting further correspondence be sent to me at my home address. So, in spite of spending almost sixteen years with the man I loved and paying a large sum of money to send him on his final journey, my requests were still ignored. I felt like I did not exist. There had been previous emails from Marlene, regarding the words for the headstone for Tosh's grave, but my suggestions did not appear to go down too well at the time. I know this was a very emotional time for all of us and these were my thoughts and feelings. I am sure it was not the intention of anyone to make me feel this way, but I did.

On this Friday night I just flipped. I no longer felt I had anything to give, to support Tosh's family. I was struggling to cope with my own grief and at this time I had feelings of loneliness, hurt, guilt and anger. All these feelings came together on this one night. I emailed Marlene and Bramwell and copied the email to Tosh's sister Sue, to cease contact with the family. I requested not to be contacted in person, by email, letter or by telephone. I needed time for me to grieve and heal. I was struggling to keep myself emotionally afloat, without the added pressures I was feeling from Tosh's family at this time. I did say that, as their FLO was not being very supportive, any information I was given by Vanessa regarding the investigation and the inquest would be passed on straightaway.

Time trundled on and everyone continued to get on with their lives, but my life was in limbo. We had not been given a date for the inquest, but indications were that it would be sometime in April. Towards the end of January, I came home from work to find a brown envelope addressed to me. I had no idea what it was, as so many brown envelopes arrived nowadays, so I wasn't concerned. I was shocked to discover it was the draft report of the investigation from British Transport Police. It was extremely detailed, regarding the performance of the train under crash conditions and also had some colour photographs of the train and Tosh's car after the crash had happened. I had not expected to see such detailed pictures. I didn't know if Vanessa was working or not, because I'd lost track of her shift patterns as we didn't need to be in contact so often. She had other families to look after besides me.

Although she never discussed other cases, or made me feel a bother or an inconvenience, I dialled her number and she answered in a couple of rings. 'Hi Luce, How are you?' 'Fine thanks,' I replied, 'I have been sent the train report today, it has some lovely colour photographs.' After checking I was alright, she was furious that this report had been sent out to me direct without prior warning, especially as it contained the photographs. She said she would speak to British Transport Police and come over to see me the next night. She made me promise to call her if I needed to chat in the meantime after reading the report. I told her not to worry, that I would be fine and we could talk tomorrow.

As the report was a draft report, it could not be shown to anyone, but I wanted Vanessa to check it over with me as they were asking if I wanted to make any amendments or comments. I was struck by the detail of the report. It had train speeds and stopping distances and they were impressed that the train had not derailed. This train had been fitted with a new special buffer, which was designed to reduce the chances of a derailment. This was the first time it had been tested under real crash conditions and it had performed well. I asked Vanessa if I could claim a fee for Tosh testing this new buffer, as a public service for the safety of future rail users. We decided this was unlikely, as Vanessa had already told me that they would be making a claim for damages to the train and the disruptions caused to rail users on that day. The current figure in mind was said to be in excess of £600,000.

Vanessa said if I wanted to make a comment on the fact that the level crossing was a half barrier, instead of a full barrier, now was my opportunity. I was told that some families use the inquests and reports as a spring board to help future campaigns to be started following the death of their loved ones. I could understand this if Tosh had been killed by a drunk driver, or if he had been hit because of a fault in road or rail safety. However, in my humble opinion, I did not feel this was applicable in his case. I had given this a lot of thought, but I was of the opinion that half barrier level crossings are safe if they are used correctly. It is the way people use them that causes the deaths, whether they are trying to jump the lights, or end their lives. I know with the barrier in question, once the lights start to flash warning you a train is approaching, there are only twenty seven seconds before the train will appear at the crossing. The barrier drops just eight seconds before the train arrives. I did not think this was very long, but it would be long enough if used correctly.

After reading the report, I went down to the train line to see the timings for myself. It is quite scary how little time there is between the flashing lights and the train crossing, but I am reliably informed this is the standard timing of a level crossing, on a minor road, in a village location.

Vanessa told me that a date had not yet been set for the inquest, but indications were that it would be sometime from April onwards. She had been told I was not required to attend, but if I wanted to go she would come with me. When Vanessa came over, to check the train report with me, she also told me she was taking some time off for study leave. She was studying to take some exams for promotion in the future. She would be away from work, from next month for few weeks, but if I needed her she said to just to give her a call. I would only call her as a last resort, as I knew her days off were much needed. With the inquest date approaching, I was still not sure how long she would be around for me.

In the beginning, I asked her how long she was assigned to me and she said it varied from family to family. In some cases she is not needed for very long at all and with others she stays in contact informally, even when they are no longer under her care. She didn't say which group I would fall into, but I knew I would miss her when she went on to help other families. I was so lucky to have her. I wanted her work to be recognised, so I wrote to the Chief Constable and the Deputy Chief Constable of Norfolk Police telling them of the invaluable support I had received from Vanessa and how I hoped her and other FLOs in Norfolk Constabulary were given the correct amount of time and backup, in order to deliver the much needed support they offered to bereaved families.

## CHAPTER FOURTEEN

A few weeks later, Vanessa called round to check on me and let me know she was going on study leave. In her hand she was waving a piece of paper. 'What have you got in you hand?' I asked. 'Are you declaring peace in our time?' 'No,' she replied, 'have you been writing letters?' I told her that I had written the letter because people only ever complain nowadays and when someone does something wonderful or outstanding it should be noted. 'I have not done anything wonderful, I was just doing my job,' she replied. I told her to shut up, 'I know from the support others have had, that you were not just doing the job, you go beyond that and I wanted it publicly noted that it does make a difference.' She admitted to me that she was initially embarrassed and her colleagues had thought that her mum had written in. 'Do I look like your Mum?' 'No,' she replied. I told her to shut up again and drink her tea. She hugged me and thanked me and we went into the lounge to catch up. The support and care I had been given by Vanessa was fantastic. It made such a difference to my mental and emotional recovery. I hoped the work of FLOs is noted as it really is appreciated, when it's done properly. From speaking to many bereaved people all around the country, I was one of the lucky ones. FLOs are not all like Vanessa and that is a terrible shame for those people they are supposed to be supporting.

Since my first conversation with Edward, we had been chatting more frequently. I would call him when I needed a friend and he would do the same when he was having a bad day. We could both chat about things that were troubling us; I was not the only one having bad days. Our friendship had gone back to the level of eighteen to twenty years ago, when we were both living in London. He had been based in Norfolk, but had requested a transfer to be nearer his wife and daughter. Living apart was not helping their marriage, which was not in great shape at this time. He was very patient with me and let me cry or rant or get angry. He just took the rough, as there was not much smooth at the time. As the inquest got nearer, he asked if I wanted him to come and support me and that he would try and get his duties moved around and be there for me. I told him how great that would be, but I did not know when it was likely to take place.

Then, out of the blue, on the ninth of March, I got a letter from the coroner's office informing me that a date had been set for the inquest and that I was required to attend as a witness. The date was set for the twentieth of March. Only eleven days time, ten if you don't count the day that the letter had arrived. I knew Vanessa was on study leave, but this was too important not to contact her and I didn't know when she was due back at work. I panicked, in case she was off still on the twentieth? I dialled the number she had given me and within a couple of rings she answered. Apologising for disturbing her, when I knew she was off duty, I explained all about the letter and read it to her. She was angry that she had not been informed and that she had not been given the list of witnesses prior to this time. Vanessa knew I had distanced myself from Tosh's family and when I said I would call them she asked if I felt comfortable enough to make the call, or if I would like her to call on my behalf? I replied that it would be fine, I would call Marlene and Bramwell with the details.

Their FLO had given them very little support and I had promised to share any information I got via Vanessa with them. Without this link they would have no clue what was happening. Vanessa was back on duty on the 19th and she promised to come over and see me sometime during that day. She also offered to visit Marlene and Bramwell, but they chose not to take up this offer. I called Marlene and gave her all the information I had been given and promised to contact them if I was advised of any changes or updates, after Vanessa had been to see me and was back from study leave. A number of telephone calls were made to Mum and Dad, Val and Edward to inform them of the date, in case they wanted to attend the inquest. All of them were worried about me and what plans I had. Vanessa had said she would take me to the inquest and stay with me throughout the day.

The Coroner had also contacted my parents a few times since Tosh's death, to check on how I was coping. He had been a friend of my mum's since they were in Youth Club together. I had babysat for his children, until I left for London to work as a nanny at eighteen. Once the inquest had been announced, he dropped in on my family to see how I was and told them if I wanted to talk to him about anything that his door was always open. Mum thanked him and explained I was being supported by Vanessa. He said he knew Vanessa well and confirmed I was in safe hands. He said he could not praise Vanessa highly enough. If she was looking after me, I would be receiving the best support available. Having been in contact with my family for so many years meant the inquest was to be led by his deputy. I did not feel I needed the contact, but it was nice to know people were thinking of me. My main support at this time came via Vanessa and Edward.

The day before the inquest Vanessa arrived at my flat. She gave me a huge hug and told me everything would be fine. She prepared me for what was due to happen. An inquest takes place when there is a sudden death, violent death or an unnatural death. The purpose of an inquest is to answer the following three questions:-

Where did the person die?
When did the person die?
How did the person die?

Because Tosh died on a live railway line, the inquest had to be held in front of a jury. The date of the inquest was largely due to having a room large enough and available for the witnesses, jury, family members and any other interested parties i.e. railway people and the press. The inquest would also decide the cause of death.

The possible causes of death for Tosh were:-
Accidental death,
Open Verdict (this is where a cause is not clear), or
Suicide.

As Tosh had left a note, the verdict in my eyes could only be suicide. Vanessa talked me through what usually happened at an inquest. Not many officers get to attend an inquest with a jury, but Vanessa had been to one before. The venue had been changed at the last minute, so she said we would plan to arrive early, so we could have a look around and she could sort out where we needed to be. She hugged me again and promised to be with me as long as I needed her the next day. The inquest was due to start at ten am, so she would pick me up between nine and nine fifteen am. She hugged me again and was gone.

The night before the inquest was one of the worst night's sleep I had had for a long time. My mind would not switch off. Since the day of the funeral my whole life had felt like it was on hold. I knew I could not afford to stay in the rented flat on a single income, so I would need to move house and buy a place of my own. I felt I could not move until after the inquest. My friends in Ireland had wanted me to take a holiday and visit them and again I could not plan anything, until I knew a date for the inquest, as I could not be in two places at once. I also wanted to plan a trip to Las Vegas to say a final goodbye to Tosh. The inquest had delayed these plans.

The very scary thing was that not having a date for the inquest gave me a handy excuse to not make plans for what I was going to do with the rest of my life. My standard answer to myself and others was 'I can't plan that until after the inquest.' Within the next twenty four hours I was going to be released from that 'comfort zone'. Despite all the support I had had from Vanessa and searching the internet, I still had no idea what was really going to happen on that day as in all the reports on the internet, only one or two had mentioned an inquest in front of a jury. It was extremely daunting.

The day arrived and I was very nervous. I had eaten some breakfast but felt really sick. I had dressed carefully, as I knew I was going to have to stand up in a room full of strangers. I was also going to meet Edward for the first time in eighteen years. We had spoken on the phone and exchanged emails, but we had not yet met up again.

Both Edward and Vanessa had said they would be there for me. Val had already booked to be at a reunion, with former staff from the supermarket chain she worked for before she retired. This get-together only happens once a year. She wanted to cancel and not attend, to be with me, but I persuaded her not to. I told her I would send her a text message when the inquest was over to let her know the outcome. I also explained that the emotions of the day may not hit me until much later and I may need her more then.

I had been so lucky in the support I had been given by Val, Vanessa and Edward. They all had different life experiences and their life situations were all so different, I was emotionally covered from all angles. These three people were the ones who got the nearest to knowing all I had survived so far. Edward had known me pre-Tosh and had experience of bereavement through his job. Vanessa had only known me for a short time, but through our time together she had known such personal details about me and my life with Tosh leading up to his death and the highs and lows I had since she had given me the news that he had died.

Her job took her to sights and places that most of us would never wish to go to or see in our lifetimes. Her compassion, personality and wisdom gained through her life so far was invaluable to me. The third member of the trio was the only one of the three to have met Tosh and seen how we had lived our lives. When times got tough for me, Val was the one who was able to remind me how far I had come and what I had lived through. She had seen Tosh before he died and the strain that his depression had taken on both of our lives. Val knows me better than I know myself in some ways.

# CHAPTER FIFTEEN

As I was preparing for this day, I began to wonder what would happen to me when the trio split up and went their separate ways. How would I cope without them? Everyone said I was doing so well. What if I cracked? I was scared to let go, in case I could not cope, so I carried on forward, hoping my mask would not slip and reveal the emotions bubbling beneath the surface.

Vanessa arrived in her dress uniform. She looked really smart. Her everyday uniform was the standard trousers and jumper. The uniform she was dressed in today was a smart jacket and trousers, highly polished boots and finished off with a police hat. I was so relieved to see her. She came and gave me a huge hug and asked how I was feeling and if I had slept at all. I told her I had not really slept at all and I felt terrible, shaky and sick. She tried to reassure me that I would be fine and was probably more nervous about meeting my friend Edward than the inquest itself. I replied that she could be right, but reiterated that we were just friends. I don't think she believed me. We went downstairs to the car. It was a plain car, not one of the brightly coloured ones.

As we drove into the city, I felt a burning sensation on the back of my legs and on my bottom. I asked Vanessa to turn back, as I did not feel at all well. She looked over at me, with a concerned look on her face, and asked me what was wrong. When I told her she burst out laughing, but continued to drive forward. I didn't see anything funny in the situation and asked her if she wanted to share the joke she was laughing about. It took a few moments for her to compose herself enough to speak, when she did she explained that the car she picked up this morning felt cold so she had put on all the heaters and the heated seat on the passenger's side to warm the car up quicker. It was a relief to know I was not ill, but simply sitting on a heated seat!

We chatted as we drove into Norwich city centre. I asked where we were going to park and Vanessa told me it was not a problem, as we were in a police car and on official duties, so we could park in the police bays in

Bethel Street. We found a space and parked up. As Vanessa was on official duties, she had to wear the hat that went with the uniform. Now it was my turn to laugh out loud. The hat that completed the uniform reminded me of the Salvation Army uniform, so I could not resist asking her where her tambourine was. It was a relief to be with someone who was in control of the situation, but who I could also share a joke with. The rapport we shared at that time, allowed us to know when we needed to laugh and when we needed to be serious. I don't think this is something you can teach someone, they have it within them. It is a very special skill Vanessa has and she is a great at judging a situation correctly, it certainly made my life easier to be with her.

When we arrived at the venue, Vanessa advised me to call Edward to see if we could meet each other again before everyone else arrived. She went off to find the coroner and work out when I would be needed and see the layout of the room. When she returned, she started looking about from side to side. 'What are you doing?' I asked her. 'Looking for Edward, is he coming?' She stood on the stairs like a naughty child jumping down a step every time the door opened, whispering 'Is it him?' 'Vanessa, you are not helping,' I told her. 'Am I not?' She replied laughing mischievously. What would I have done without her?

When he arrived, he walked over and gave me a massive hug and asked how I was feeling. I stepped back and said I was fine.

When Edward was first back in contact, he noticed I had two standard replies to the question, 'How are you feeling?'. The reply on a bad day was 'fine' and on stronger days the reply would be 'ok'.

I introduced him to Vanessa and she said 'Hello, pleased to meet you at last.' They both said they had heard lots about each other and that it was good to finally meet. It would have been great to have Val there to complete the trio, but it was not going to happen. Vanessa told us to disappear and try and relax and be back here in fifteen minutes, as she wanted to show me the room before it started.

Fifteen minutes did not give us long enough to go for a coffee, so we went outside for a chat. Edward was dressed in a suit and tie, with an overcoat over his arm. He was incredibly overdressed, but he said his uniform would have been too much, jeans would have been too casual, and he did not want to scare people with the clerical collar. We chatted briefly, before we were joined by Tosh's sister, Sue, and her partner, Roger. I had never given my friendship with Edward much thought, we had been friends for so long. He was an old friend who was helping me more than he will ever know. But Sue's reaction when I introduced them stopped me in my tracks. He was introduced as an old friend. I did not see it as important to explain he was an ordained member of clergy in the Church of England and that he was married with a teenage daughter. It did not seem important to us, he was just Edward to me and was a very loyal friend. Sue saw it differently. Whether she meant to show her thoughts or not, I am not sure. Edward noticed it and after he had been introduced he explained we had know each other since we had been in Youth Club together and became friends when we were in London at the same time about twenty years ago. He then went on to explain he was a chaplain in the RAF and married with a thirteen year old daughter.

Tosh's sister visibly relaxed at the mention of a wife and daughter and being a man of the cloth just sealed it for her. I am guessing her first thoughts were that it had not taken Lucy long to recover from her brother's death and replace him with this handsome man. She was wrong on so many levels. Firstly, I had not recovered from Tosh's death. Also friendship with Edward was the only level we were on. He was married and had never given any indication we were going to be anything but friends during the whole time we had known each other. Sue and Roger went inside and I apologised to Edward for her distant welcome. He said it was not a problem and I was not to worry. He went on to explain it was going to be an emotional day for all of us and her thoughts were of her brother, not me, hence he felt that a reason to clarify our friendship.

We went inside and were greeted by my twin and her husband, my Dad (Mum was on school run standby for my twin's children in case the inquest went on longer than expected). Vanessa came forward and took me to one side to show me the room and explain what was due to happen. The coroner had planned to sit all the witnesses in order, starting with me as the first witness. This would mean I would be sitting at the far end of the room, away from my family and support. Vanessa said this would not be happening and arranged for me to be sat at the other end nearer to my family. The coroner also explained that the witnesses would be called one by one and asked to read out their statements. Vanessa was well aware by this time that my fear of talking to strangers on a one-to-one basis would have been difficult for me, but to stand up and speak to a room full of strangers, including the jury, about my life with Tosh was beyond me at this point in my life.

Vanessa did not make a huge issue out of this to embarrass me, but explained that this was not going to be possible for me to do at this time, with all the emotions of the day. She spoke to the coroner and a change of plan was put in place. The coroner agreed to read out the statement and I would comment occasionally, to confirm the details being read out were correct.

Everyone entered the room. The jury were led in and were seated. The room had a large table surrounded by chairs in the centre and wooden pews, similar to those found in a church around the edges. The jury sat on one side, the witnesses sat opposite. My family and support sat opposite the coroner. Representatives of the railway company and the union rep sat with the reporter from the local newspaper, next to the jury in line with my family. Sue and Roger elected to sit at the table in the centre.

I sat next to a couple, who it turned out had been sitting in their car at the level crossing and saw the whole thing unfold before their very eyes. To my other side sat Vanessa. As we all stood for the coroner to enter the room, Vanessa leaned over and squeezed my hand in support and whispered to ask if I was ok. I think I whispered back that I was ok and returned the squeeze of her hand.

The proceedings began with the swearing in of the jury and the coroner explaining the purpose of an inquest. The first witness was called and with another quick squeeze from Vanessa I was sworn in and asked to confirm my name and address. The coroner then began reading my statement that Vanessa had taken from me, back in November, which seemed like an age ago but was in fact only five months ago. After confirming my name and address, I corrected the coroner regarding Tosh's name. His name was Darrell Sheens, but she was intent on dropping the 's'. The rest of the statement charted my life with Tosh and the weeks and days leading to his death. It felt very emotional to listen to the personal details of my life read out. I had retold the story of our lives so many times to our reunited families, but it was quite unsettling to hear it again in such an unfamiliar arena.

# CHAPTER SIXTEEN

When my part was complete, I went back to my seat. Vanessa nudged me to ask if I was alright, her eyes were full of concern and kindness and she held my hand for the rest of the proceedings. Her thoughtfulness and compassion could not be faulted, knowing she was there made such a difference. I doubt anyone else would have noticed this was happening. She was discreet, professional and I knew whatever happened I would never be able to repay her kindness to me. If I had been given anyone else as an FLO, I don't think I would have received such support and thoughtfulness. I had long ceased to see her as a policewoman and felt we were friends. I hoped I had not read the situation wrongly, as I would miss her presence in my life when she left.

The other witnesses all followed the same pattern that I set out. Statements were read and confirmed by the witnesses to be correct. At the inquest I learned that Tosh had spent some time down by the railway crossing on the day he wrote my 'Goodbye Lucy' letter. Witnesses included people who had seen him the week before his death, the couple in the car waiting to cross the level crossing, the train driver and other passengers from the train. Once all the details were heard, the jury left to make their decision. Vanessa led me away to a coffee shop downstairs from the room we were in. My family followed and chose a table with Tosh's sister Sue and her partner Roger, who they were familiar with. Vanessa was a stranger to them. Edward came with me and Vanessa. We were joined by the men from the British Transport Police who had completed the investigation. It was good to finally meet them and put names to faces, as Vanessa introduced the people round the table. I was on the verge of a panic attack, chatting to so many strangers, but my 'Equity card' came in handy and with a good bit of acting I am sure nobody was aware there was anything wrong.

Always the gentleman, Edward went to buy the teas and coffees, but this was Vanessa's duty and she paid for our drinks. Vanessa kept the conversation flowing until it was time to return. Before we went back in, Vanessa took me aside to check I was still breathing and asked if I was prepared for whatever I was about to hear. I told her I was not sure about prepared, but I was not going to be surprised if the verdict was announced as suicide. In my own mind that was all it could be. I said I would be upset if we got an open verdict, as this would mean they could not decide on a cause of death and this would be no answer at all.

We returned to the room. We were all asked to stand for the return of the coroner. The jury was asked if they had reached a verdict. 'Yes,' the jury spokesman replied. The verdict was read out as suicide. Vanessa touched my arm to check I was ok. I replied that I was and tried to raise a smile. Tosh's sister dropped to the floor as the verdict was announced. She was attended to and given something to drink. As we left the room, Vanessa pulled me to one side. She'd been asked by the reporter if I wanted to make a statement; she assured me that I was under no obligation. I knew instinctively that I didn't want to say anything, but needed to speak to Tosh's sister, as she was his family. We both agreed we did not wish to comment and this was fed back to the reporter. Vanessa asked what plans I had for the rest of the day, adding that her time had been booked out so if I wanted to spend time with her, or be driven anywhere, the choice was mine. She would go with whatever I wanted, depending on how I was feeling. Also, my brother-in-law had said there was room in their car, if I wanted to go back with him and the family. So I decided to spend time with my sister and her family and release Vanessa to more worthy police work, rather than babysitting me.

Before we left, I went and had a word with Tosh's sister to check she was alright and to ask her to let her family know I was thinking of them, but still needed some time for me. She told me they understood but wanted me to know they were there when I felt ready to contact them again and she said she I hoped one day I would. During the time for me, I had worked out I could not afford to maintain the flat I was living in and the solution was to use some of the insurance money as a deposit to buy a house of my own. I had found a house and I showed Tosh's sister and Edward the details I had in my handbag. Vanessa joined us as the house discussions continued, until we were gently moved to the door, as they wanted to lock up behind us.

As we got to the entrance lobby, we all exchanged hugs and kisses and went our separate ways. Edward hugged me and promised to be in touch.

Vanessa did likewise, reminding me that her phone was on if I needed her. I thanked her for everything she had done for me and I left with my family. When I got in the car, I sent a text message to Val to let her know what the verdict was and told her how wonderful Vanessa had been and that I would call her in a few days time. Wanting to set her mind at rest, I told her she should relax and enjoy her reunion and that I was with my sister and her family, so not alone, and she was not to worry about me.

I got back to my Mum's house and we sat round the kitchen table to discuss the details and what had happened. We then heard Elvis singing 'Suspicious Minds.' Then I remembered one of the boys at work had helped me download this as my ring tone on my mobile phone for me. 'Phone!' Everyone shouted at once. It was Vanessa. 'Hello Vanessa, how are you?' 'Fine thanks, Luce,' she was just calling to tell me the text message I had sent to Val had actually been sent to her by mistake. Their names were next to each other in my phone book. 'Good job I didn't say anything bad about you,' I laughingly replied. I thanked her again for all she had done for me during that day. She, as usual, told me that it was not a problem and, if I needed her, I knew where to find her. I resent the message to Val and rejoined the family group.

Our group had to break up when my sister had to leave and get the children from school. I telephoned the office to let them know what had happened and that I would be back to work the next day. They told me that if I needed more time off it was not a problem, but I thought I would be fine and that right now I was with my sister and her family so I was not on my own at least. The rest of the day was spent being Auntie Lucy, which was a great way to end what was a very emotional day.

My Life Changing Moment

## CHAPTER SEVENTEEN

When I returned to work the next day I realised the newspaper and television coverage of the verdict had upset more people than the death itself. I had not given the word suicide much thought before, but I was forced to give it some thought now. Intelligent, educated people began to avoid me like I had a disease. I think they felt uncomfortable, somehow believing that if they were in contact with me the same might happen to them. The curious wanted to know the details. What had happened at the inquest? Was it as portrayed on television? I felt like I was living in a goldfish bowl. Some of the looks and glances I got were of pity, 'that poor girl, her other half committed suicide.' Others wanted to know if I felt guilty. Why did I not try to stop him?

During the months that led to Tosh's death, I had not told anyone of the stress and worry we were dealing with. I did not want to admit we were failing and not able to cope. He had suffered from incredible lows but up to that point together we had coped, as I was able to lift him back to normal and life continued. One night, he suffered a panic attack and he felt he could not breathe. We dialled 999, not knowing what else to do and a paramedic arrived in a four by four vehicle, closely followed by an ambulance. He was stabilised by the paramedic and we drove to the emergency doctor at the hospital, to get him some tablets to help him through the night. The next day he had booked an appointment at the doctors to ask for counselling, to help him with the depression he was suffering. The doctor just gave him antidepressants that he never took. That same day, I had an interview for promotion and all was going well, until the question of flexibility came up. I was asked if I would be flexible in my working hours. I said at the moment for personal reasons I could not.

I did not want to leave Tosh if he hit a low, in case I could not lift him again, but I was too proud to give my reasons. I was working hard to prove I could do the job, as I was carrying it out as a temporary promotion, but I was just doing the minimum hours for fear of leaving him longer than necessary. I felt I was juggling Tosh and work. Tosh was always my top priority and work had to be secondary for the moment. It was not my news to share, and I felt if I spoke out I would be letting Tosh down on the loyalty stakes, so I said nothing. I missed out on my promotion.

So when people ask me, do I feel guilty or could I have done more to help him, I know without a doubt my answer would be 'no.' He was my priority above all else. No one knew what we had lived through together, or for how long, because we coped alone. Val knew Tosh was ill because she had seen how he had lost weight and lost colour. But even Val was not aware how low he had got. It is a very personal struggle and very few people in the same situation would have spoken out and told people what was going on. The first time anyone knew something was not quite right was the Friday before he died. He had hit a low in the middle of the day and I had to ask for permission to leave work and help him. It was then that I broke down in tears, when I was questioned why I needed to go. Even then I did not know he would take his own life only two days later. I think it was a shock to many people that this could happen to someone they knew and they had not known what was happening, or do anything to help us. Again, not everyone was privy to this information, if they were they would not be asking such stupid questions.

I work in Personnel so these people are supposed to be caring and sensitive people. It just shows how wrong you can be and it was around this time I began to see who my possible true friends could be. They were the ones who did not immediately come out with an insensitive question. One question some did ask was 'what did a verdict at an inquest really mean?' This was an easy one to answer! It meant I could be issued a full and final death certificate and tie up lots of loose ends with regards to Tosh's estate. When I did get the full death certificate it had to be reissued, as they had mistyped the place of death, but eventually I had the final certificate.

Vanessa had visited me to check I was alright. This was one of the final duties she had as my FLO before she disappeared to help other families. It was in the coming months that I was to discover if I would be one of the families Vanessa ceased to visit, or if we would become friends. I hoped it was the latter. My feelings were that we had become friends, but it was not up to me, it was Vanessa's call if she chose to change from FLO to friend.

Some of the paperwork given back to me was the service history of the car and the MOT certificate for the car Tosh destroyed. I was also surprised to be given the tax disc back. It had been blackened at the edges but it was readable. I did not know what to do with it so I sent it to DVLA in Swansea with a covering note explaining about the disc and Tosh's death. I was even more surprised to receive a refund for the unused tax as the car had been recorded as off the road.

I then contacted the car insurance people to explain about the outcome of the inquest and ask if there was any further paperwork they needed from me to finalise everything their end. The man on the other end of the phone said he was aware of the outcome of the inquest, via the train company that had put in a claim for damages. It meant this claim would be open for three years to give people a chance to put in a claim if they needed to. I asked if there was an amount being claimed currently against the policy and I was told I could not be given an exact figure, as the claim was ongoing, but I was told it was in excess of six hundred thousand pounds. I asked how this was going to be settled and he explained that he was going to use the car insurance policy for the car Tosh was driving when the incident happened. As the policy was fully comprehensive he could see no problem. I then asked, as the inquest had found the death to be suicide, would that make the policy invalid? As the small print on most insurance policies states that, if a claim was found to be deliberate, then the policy becomes invalid.

Suicide sounded fairly deliberate to me. However, I was told that the phrase was included within insurance policies so that if someone decides they simply want a new car, the insurance company has the discretion to not pay out. The example I was given was, that if someone drove into a wall to write their car off that would be deliberate. The man continued that Tosh had not done this to gain from the policy and, therefore, the policy was still valid. This was such a relief to me, if it was invalid then the claim could be made against Tosh's estate, which was effectively me. I could not even begin to contemplate how I would deal with a bill for such a large sum. So, no further paperwork was required until the claim would be closed around November 2008.

My life returned to what was now meant to be normal and I had to make plans to decide what I wanted to do with the rest of my life. I chose to take each day as it came and build on that. My support team had changed and moved on. Vanessa had moved on to new families and although we have remained in contact now as friends, the support was now a two-way thing. I no longer had the priority due to having a crisis; she had bad days too and felt comfortable enough to lean on me and cry on my shoulder. I in turn was able to be there to support her when she needed a friend.

## CHAPTER EIGHTEEN

Edward and I met up for a meal and to chat over old times. We talked about our youth and remembered Sunday school outings that all seemed to run so smoothly, with a trip to a stretch of Norfolk coastline, then a stop on the way home for a picnic of sandwiches, iced buns and packets of Iced Gems. He recalled the surprise when we got to the picnic sites, or the beaches, with games of beach football or cricket. I admitted I saw it a little differently. The trips seemed to me just an extension of the Reynolds family Sunday outings we'd had, in order to check opening times and space for the coach to stop and location of toilets and running water for the picnics. My Mum was the Sunday school teacher for over thirty years, so all the planning and praise goes to her! Always the night before the Sunday school outings or Sunday school parties, the kitchen table was taken over by sandwich making and old ice cream tubs were transformed into carriers for strawberry or orange flavoured jellies.

We reminisced about our youth club days, with rounders being played on the church meadow. The route, to run from base to base, was determined by where the cowpats were placed in the field. We also remembered a retreat we had been on at Coltishall, with one of the lasting memories of that weekend being raft building, or in our case the raft sinking and the evenings spent at the local pub!

When I went to work in London as a nanny I knew no-one and, while in my new surroundings, telephone numbers were passed via our parents and Edward and I made contact again. His girlfriend was still back in Norwich, so we both needed a friend, to meet up and share a drink or two, to let off steam and chat over old times. I had also joined Holy Trinity Church in Brompton during my time in London, but I don't recall if Edward ever joined me there.

Eventually, time moved on and I returned to Norfolk. I celebrated my twenty first birthday with my twin and our younger sister Kath joined in the celebrations to mark her fifteenth birthday. A barn dance was a great way for everyone to join in and helped mix the different age groups included in our family and friends. A great time was had by all!

It was at this time I did feel more for Edward than I was letting him know, but he was now engaged and seemed happy in his life. The next time we met was at his wedding and as one of his closest friends I wished him happiness and he went off to his life and I went off to mine.

After the meal we walked back to our cars and admitted how different our lives would have been if we had been more than friends twenty years ago. We both admitted that we did feel like being more than friends back then, but we were both afraid of rejection. Edward has said nothing because he was frightened of losing a great friend if I did not feel the same. I had given away no clues to my feelings then. Now, I admitted I had said nothing because he had told me he was happy and getting married - I was not about to steal another girl's man. Besides, I never knew he thought of me in that way. It's funny how life turns out, if things had been different I would never have met Tosh and Edward would not have had a wonderful daughter. So everything works out for the best sometimes.

Edward also confided in me that he was having a few hiccups in his marriage and asked if he could say in touch, as it helped him to talk to someone who had known him so long and he felt comfortable sharing his worries with me. I must admit I needed his friendship too and we shared further meals and walks during the summer. He had requested a posting nearer his family, to make a concerted effort at making the marriage work and we stayed in contact until he was posted.

We then decided that, if his marriage was going to work, he would need to concentrate on his family. We agreed that staying in regular contact was just confusing and upsetting for both of us. Exchanging numbers and addresses for emergency contact only we parted company. It was not until Edward was out of my life again that I realised what I really felt for him, but it was too late and I had to move on with my life without him, again.

We remained in contact via Christmas cards. Unfortunately his marriage ended in divorce but both Edward and his ex-wife now have new partners and seem happy. His engagement was announced and I wish him much happiness in his future life.

I can never repay Edward for his friendship and support at a time when I needed it most. I wish he had got the chance to have met Val, for at the time their paths never crossed. I would have liked the trio of Val, Vanessa, and Edward to have met, as between them they have helped me through some of the most emotional days of my life in one way or another.

It is often said people will come into your life for a reason, a season or a lifetime. Only time will tell which one of the trio was the season or the reason or the lifetime. I am just glad that they were all there for me.

# CHAPTER NINETEEN

Val remained my constant support and I began to get to know my younger sister Katherine too. When I had left the family Kath was still at school and I had missed all of her adult years so far. I had not got the chance to know her before really. We had meals together at my flat and went out for drinks as we got to know one another. Since I had been gone Kath had got married to Peter who I hadn't known before, but we got on straightaway. With Kath I am able to be myself, she has been there when I have needed a friend and we are now really close. So much good has come from one man's death.

As the summer wore on, I had been for a break to stay with my friends in Ireland and returned to find the house I was in the process of buying was built on a flood plain and I would struggle to get affordable home insurance, if at all. I had no choice with a limited budget so had to pull out.

I felt that I had grown up during this time and ready to make contact with Tosh's family once again. I was welcomed back with open arms. I hoped they understood why I needed that time alone to recover from Tosh's death and the pain and grief I was coping with. I would hate to think I had hurt them again when they were so vulnerable. I am now welcomed as part of the Sheens family and my feelings towards them are of love and friendship... and I hope they continue to feel the same about me.

One of the things I wanted to do was to travel to Las Vegas. I had been to the railway line, to his graveside and to some of the places we had lived and visited together, but nowhere could I feel Tosh around me. Las Vegas was our place. I had made up my mind that I wanted to go and lay to rest any ghosts that were still present. I thought a good time to go would be straight after the first anniversary of his death, so that when I returned it would be a fresh start in a new year. This had been on my mind for a long while, but until the inquest was over I didn't want to book a trip anywhere. Now I could, so I booked the flight and then called Las Vegas and booked the hotel direct. This was something to look forward to. Family and friends thought I was mad to go alone, but I just booked it, saying it was not a problem.

Just after my house purchase fell through I seemed to lose direction a little and my life seemed to hit a rut. I was not feeling like I was in control of anything. My weight had gone up and I felt under pressure. People assumed I would recover from the inquest, meet someone new and life would go on. You should do this, or do that. Grow your hair in this style. Have you done this yet? Have you been to this place? Why are you wearing those jeans, they do nothing for you? Have you chased this house or that house? It felt as if everyone knew the best way – their way, or the highway! The only thing I knew I could control was my haircut. I was fed up of well meaning people telling me what I should do. I was feeling pressured and my confidence was ebbing away fast.

So I planned to have my head shaved. The more people that said don't do it, the more stubborn and determined to do it I became. I had an appointment booked at the hairdressers for a Thursday lunchtime. All morning I got the comments, 'Lucy, don't do it, just have a trim, your hair is so lovely.' By twelve, I had made up my mind. I got to the hairdressers and asked for the clippers. 'What number comb are we using?' I was asked. 'Number six, please,'

I answered. Number one comb was designed to cut the shortest. My hair began to fall to the floor. In the mirror I could see two elderly ladies waiting under the dryers. Their faces were so shocked when this hair came off. As each clump of hair fell to the floor my confidence returned. I loved it. When it was finished I asked the hairdresser to go over it again with the number four comb. I felt liberated and the best I had felt in a long time. I went home and showered the old bits of hair off, retouched my makeup and returned to work. I looked stunning and felt wonderful.

Lots of people did a second look when they saw me but most said it did suit me. Lots of them said I was very brave. It struck me they said I was brave to have my hair shaved off, but I had not been called brave when I was widowed by suicide. How strange is life sometimes?

Another change in my appearance was more out of my control. The following night I was eating a cookie at home when I heard a crack and realised the oatmeal and raisin cookie that should have been soft was in fact hard and I had snapped off my two front teeth. This is not as dramatic as it sounds, as my two front teeth were on a plate so not mine at all. I stopped munching, took out the teeth, finished the cookie and then removed the plate. I knew my dentist had emergency surgery on a Saturday morning so I did not foresee a problem and went to bed, setting the alarm to get to the dentist nice and early. When I got to the dentist, I was told that nothing could be done until Monday because the lab does not work at the weekend.

I was due to view houses with Mum and Dad on the Sunday. I had not yet plucked up the courage to return to church, so met Mum and Dad at home. Dad was in the garden and Mum was not home yet. The first thing Dad said was, 'that's a smart hair cut.' When I opened my mouth to smile he looked and burst out laughing, 'wait 'til mum sees you like that, you'll be for it.' When Mum arrived she looked at the hair and put her head in her hands, 'What have you done?' Dad immediately dropped me in it, saying 'You haven't seen the best bit yet!' I smiled and Mum nearly cried. 'Lucy, you haven't been fighting have you?' When I saw my five year old niece later in the day she said 'Don't worry Auntie Lucy, they will grow back and if you put them in a tooth bag and under your pillow, the tooth fairy will bring you some money!' She was right about them growing back. By Monday night they were fixed and back as good as new, but I am still waiting for the tooth fairy!

Being accepted back as part of the family, by most of the family, has made me appreciate how important a role they play. As children, we were taken out to the beach in the summer and on holidays to Scotland, where Dad left his raincoat at the top of Edinburgh Castle, and the Isle of Wight, where a donkey ate my sister's flip flop at Carisbrooke Castle; also, riding the snails in Joyland in Great Yarmouth and having bags of pennies to put in the slot machines.

Whenever Dad used to take us out for a 'mystery tour' it always seemed to end up as a dead end or in a farmyard. Having spent more and more time with my family makes me aware of how much family time I missed out on. It makes me realise how much most of us take our families for granted, until they are not around, whether this is due to family disagreements or something more permanent. I am lucky I have a second chance…not everyone gets that second chance.

So many people had asked me how I outwardly accepted Tosh's death so easily. They wanted to know what counselling I had had or was I part of a bereavement support group. I had never considered either of these options, I had just worked through my feelings as they came up. I had been living with Tosh's depression for a lot longer than most people had been aware so I knew in my own mind that I had done all I could to help him. I had looked on the internet at various websites that dealt with suicide after he had died, but none of them had the thoughts or feelings of the families left behind. They mainly explained about the suicidal person and how to help them when they were on a downward spiral. These internet sites would not have helped us had we known about them before. I never knew that Tosh was suicidal, as he had not tried to take his life before, or mentioned the thought of taking his life.

I had watched programmes on television of people suffering from bi polar, or manic depression, which is an extreme form. They showed some of the characteristics I had seen in Tosh: obsessive behaviour, being a perfectionist, antisocial with outsiders. It showed me that the life we had shared was similar to lots of families where a family member has depression. I learned that the depressed person will have many highs and lows. The highs in Tosh's depression were shown by the enthusiasm to start a new hobby or project. When Tosh had one of these ideas, nothing would stop him from seeing it through, whether it was a new house move, planning a holiday, or learning a new skill (like Poker in his final years). Looking back, I can see that the lows were masked by these ideas or plans. If he had not had another plan in place, his low points may have been apparent and exposed before. I am not certain he was even aware of the highs and lows over the years himself. If he was, he never mentioned it.

During my life with Tosh he was always the dominant person in our relationship. He was eight years older than me, which seemed to have a certain influence, and so we did things his way. If he said something was to be done a certain way, I never thought to question it, as nine times out of ten he would be right. If I did do something my way, it did seem to go wrong and he would correct it. This did nothing for my confidence.

In Tosh's eyes there was no right or wrong, just his way. He would have such stubborn ideas: what brands of food we ate, what clothes he would wear or where he would shop. His opinions were so strong; I lost the ability to think for myself. We tried once to prove the point. I said I wanted to help him more, so he agreed we could go food shopping. He gave me the list and said he was going to leave it to me and he was going to be in charge of the trolley. It was hopeless, my lack of confidence over making choices, even if it was which brand of baked beans to buy, was so bad I was paralysed and could not pick a tin from the shelf, for fear of it being the wrong one. It took forever to walk around the supermarket. He said when we got home that it did not matter if I picked the wrong one, we would still eat them, but I am not so sure this would have been the case. His manner and authority meant we never shopped together again.

Another example of his stubbornness or dominant personality was when I used the wrong tea towel. It was only a small thing, but the consequences were uncomfortable and upsetting. In one of our rented houses we had no space for a washing line, so Tosh fixed an indoor drying rail from the ceiling in one of the spare bedrooms. He was obsessed with rotating everything, whether it was a plate or cup in the kitchen cupboard, or towels, sheets and clothing in the wardrobes. I bet I was the only person working in my office whose partner did the washing and ironing and then rotated the clothes, even my underwear!

One day I had been washing some dishes and could not find the tea towel, so went upstairs to the spare room to fetch it. The breeze was blowing through, so Tosh had hung it on the rail to dry between meal times. I grabbed the nearest one and continued downstairs. I thought I was helping. Within ten minutes Tosh was in the kitchen, shouting and ranting about the tea towel. How stupid could I have been? I had picked up the clean one he had just washed, rather than the one delegated to be used in the kitchen at the time.

I could not see what the problem was, but it was going to upset his rotation of the laundry. After about twenty minutes of shouting he calmed down to silence. The silence lasted for three days and it was an uncomfortable silence. The silence also increased Tosh's dominance and made me feel I was stupid for not seeing and understanding his 'logic'.

At the time my confidence was so low that I began to believe that I was the one who was stupid or irrational. When you are in that situation, it is very difficult to believe your own self-worth.

Anyone who said I was an idiot to stay in such a relationship cannot have been in that situation before themselves, or they would have understood how it feels and not voiced that opinion. It's like being under a spell and it takes a great deal of courage to walk away or change it from within.

I don't believe Tosh was a bad person, but he had a firm idea on how his life should be lived and these were not always clear to outsiders, or even me sometimes. I must admit that I still rotate sheets and towels, but not clothing or crockery. This must prove there is a rebel inside me somewhere!

His opinions were strong on everything we tackled. I finally decided I could not face another house move and voiced my thoughts during the summer of 2005. We had moved nineteen times in the fifteen plus years we had been together. Building from scratch, renovating, extending houses we bought and living in rented accommodation in between projects.

I noticed Tosh hit a low when we sold our final project and we decided we could not continue with moving house every six months to a year, as it was wearing me down. This meant there would be no new project to lift his low and he had no way of lifting himself, or knowing how to change his mood or mindset. I have no way of knowing if I had said no to a house move in previous years whether he would have taken the same course of action, but whilst we were healthy and financially strong it did not seem to be a problem moving again. I also feel he had been given his own way so I could have a peaceful life for many years, which probably compounded the issue when I decided I could not face a further house move. I don't remember saying no to him before, to any plan or project in the past, so I have no way of knowing what difference this might have made.

## CHAPTER TWENTY

During the summer of soul searching, a friend of the family contacted my mum. He had heard what had happened and offered to meet me for a coffee and a chat if I wanted to talk. I had known this man and his wife since my teenage years and they were friends of my parents. I dialled his number and we arranged to meet up. He came to the flat and I offered him coffee and we hugged, as he asked me how I was doing. I said I was fine. His wife had committed suicide thirteen years earlier. He said you can be honest with me, how are you really feeling? I explained that most of the time I am coping ok, other times not so good. This was the first time I had spoken to someone who had lost their life partner to suicide. His wife had attempted suicide many times and during our conversation we identified many similarities in behaviour. These included panic attacks and obsessive behaviour. For example, not being able to go to bed until the house was tidy, not being able to leave ironing or washing up. One of Tosh's worries towards the end of his life was wondering how we would get the washing dry in a one bedroom flat. He was not thinking of the big things, like not being able to afford to buy a house of our own.

Routine was also very important to our partners and it was a real eye opener to speak to someone else who had been through the stress of depression and the grief of a death through suicide. It really helped to listen to the thoughts and feelings of someone else and it felt like for the first time I was not the only one and not going through this alone, others had been there before me. After the meeting, I began to trawl the internet and this eventually led to contact with a lady called Jacqui. She had started an online support group for those who had been widowed by suicide. As I had never married, I was not sure I could join. However, she said if I had lost my life partner to suicide then the pain was the same and I was classed in her eyes as a widow.

The group is a closed group to protect our confidentiality. We can post our hopes and fears without being judged, knowing we have all been widowed by suicide. The group is in its early stages, but already those of us that are further down the road of grief are able to share our experiences to help the newly bereaved that are joining us. It is such a help to know we are not alone in our struggles and worries. We share postings of good days and bad days and it helps all of us. They say a problem shared is a problem halved and in this case it proves to be true. There are not many places to discuss bereavement by suicide, without being judged and we are all very grateful to Jacqui for setting up this place for us who need it.

The group is in its early stages, but eventually we would love to expand this so others who need our support can find us. It's a very delicate balancing act of keeping us confidential so we can be open and frank about our worries and questions, but making it available to more people who need our support. We are hoping at some point to gain charitable status, because opening ourselves up to more people would need an expansion that could not be funded by one person. Those who have found us have felt the support and gone on to support the newly bereaved that have joined us. Thanks again Jacqui, be proud of yourself and what you have achieved to date.

Another big step was finding a new home to purchase. I had searched house after house. I was just beginning to lose hope of finding something in my price range when a three bedroom modern semi-detached came up for sale. I went to view it with Mum and Dad, (it is not safe or sensible to view a property alone, so I always took someone with me, I have found brothers-in-law are handy to take property viewing too) and immediately felt I had found my home. I put an offer in and this was accepted. Solicitors were instructed and I just had to hope and pray all would be well.

Talking of praying, I finally felt worthy enough to return to church. I was made to feel welcome straight away. It was a lovely feeling to go to church and take communion with my family again, after so long away. When I felt I needed a lift it really helped me. Some people thought I had been travelling or at university but had they thought how long I had been away they would have realised that the only university course that long was the university of life. Going back to church had the added element of making conversation with people. I was still having panic attacks about being in a social conversation with strangers and making conversation after church forced me out of my comfort zone. It helped me to talk to people and gain confidence. I am improving every week.

I was coping so well. The planning of the house move and the planning of the holiday were in full swing, but then one Thursday morning driving into work I heard on the local news another man had died, on the same level crossing as Tosh. I got to work and called Mum and Dad to ask them if they had heard any more details, as they listened to the local radio station over breakfast. All the details they had heard were the same and that another man had died. I put it to the back of my mind and continued with my day. I went to the supermarket to do my food shopping after work on my way home and the local evening paper had the death on the front page. It also had pictures of Tosh's death and named Tosh as another man who had died on the line. I called Marlene and Bramwell to warn them, in case they had not heard. They had not had an evening paper and had been out all day, so had not been aware of the day's happenings. I warned them in case seeing the details opened old wounds for them. I did a quick shop and got home to find a message on the answer phone from Mum, warning me that Tosh's picture had been used on the lunchtime news.

I turned on the television and watched the ITV local news and they were kind enough to show the footage about Tosh's death and all the details once more. I then watched the BBC local news they were more discreet and only reported that this was another death on the line and they did not name Tosh at all. I got a text from Marlene and Bramwell thanking me for warning them and they had time to warn other family members. They also reassured me they were fine and let me know that if I needed them I knew where they were. The whisky bottle took a hammering and I cried and grieved again for Tosh and spared thoughts for the other poor family suffering the loss of their loved one. The details that were released at this early stage said that witnesses thought the man was trying to jump the crossing, rather than it being a suspected suicide.

The next day, the newspapers were filled with the accident and Tosh's photo and details. I went to read a friend's paper to see what was being said. I could not believe they could just print Tosh's details without letting the family know, so I contacted the government department that deals with data protection. This is an act brought in to protect sensitive data and how it can be used, stored and reprinted. I was told the only person who could make a complaint was Tosh. Data protection does not cover a deceased person or the family left behind and the only way to stop them reprinting his details again was to appeal to the better nature of the television company or the newspaper. I could not believe this was the case! As soon as you die, you lose all rights of protection. The family and I had to pick ourselves up and begin again. It was a shock to see everything in print again, but there was nothing we could do but be there for each other. I know the media just want to report news and sell papers, but often they give very little thought to how their actions affect other people.

The paperwork for my new home was coming through thick and fast and I needed to give a month's notice to my landlady to hand back the rented flat. Once I exchanged contracts, I knew the house purchase was certain and gave my notice to vacate the flat. I was able to get the keys to my new home a week before moving out of the flat, so I could move in at my leisure. I got the keys and took my twin for the first look round my new home. This was my first home purchase alone and it was exciting and scary. When we got to the house, Mum and Dad were parked on the road with a homemade cake and a bottle of wine and some plastic cups to seal the deal. My sister spent the weekend helping me clean the house, in preparation for moving in a week later. I spent my evenings driving to the new house taking boxes of small stuff and placing them in my new home. It felt very strange to be putting my things in my new house, knowing no-one was going to say 'don't put that there', 'why are you hanging that picture there, or putting the crockery in that cupboard, or on that shelf.' A van was borrowed and the moving day arrived. Mum, Dad, Mum's brother, my twin and her husband all arrived to lend a hand. My brother-in-law worked with me to lift and move the heavier items and my new home was taking shape. The first night alone was no problem at all. I was exhausted and after checking the doors were locked and the windows were closed several times, I drifted off to sleep.

The next day for me was one of the most emotional days I had experienced since Tosh's death and I was not prepared for it. To me it was just another Saturday. I was going to clean the flat ready to hand back the keys to the landlady. I arrived mid-morning and had not had time for breakfast so I went to the bakery in the village to buy some bread and cake to reward myself for my hard work. This bakery was where Tosh had bought our bread and treats. I bought some bread and an afghan, which is a large chocolate biscuit covered in chocolate coating. I had a bottle of water and made my way back to the flat. The flat was empty except my cleaning things and the hoover. I thoroughly cleaned the bathroom and kitchen, before allowing myself to have a break. I sat on the lounge floor had a large slurp of water and settled down to eat my afghan. The quiet of the flat and the taste of the afghan brought back memories of Tosh and the life we had shared in this flat. I was thinking of the worry and stress of Tosh's depression since moving to this place. I suddenly began to feel very alone and had no idea how I was going to rebuild my life without him. The loneliness and grief began to engulf me. I just sat there and sobbed, the tears flowed and my whole body shook. I put my head in my hands and cried like I had never cried before, I was inconsolable. This wave of sadness and grief happened so suddenly that I did not have time to put my guard up. I couldn't stop shaking and crying. I was scaring myself, but I could not change what was happening. After about half an hour, the tears subsided and I began to regain my composure. I still felt extremely alone, but more together than I had been a few minutes before. I spoke out loud to Tosh and told him I loved him and I missed him and I hoped he was peaceful. I went on to tell him about my new home and my forthcoming trip to Las Vegas. I finished my cookie and washed it down with a bit more water. I was then refreshed and got up and finished my cleaning. I washed the parts of the carpets that needed it, removing the remaining marks that Vanessa had left where she sat at my feet, almost a year ago to the day. When I had finished the flat was spotless. I had closed the flat and the door on memories I had of the time I had lived there. The next time I would enter the flat would be to hand back the keys to the landlady, in a couple of day's time.

## CHAPTER TWENTY ONE

The rest of the day was spent food shopping and unpacking the remaining boxes. The following day was Remembrance Sunday and one day short of the first anniversary of Tosh's death. The whole service at church seemed to be based around remembering loved ones who had died. It was an emotional service for me with thoughts of Tosh's death uppermost in my mind. I made it through the day with a few tears, thoughts of the past year and what had happened on that Sunday one year ago.

I was asked if I wanted to take the day off as leave on the thirteenth of November 2006, but I said I would be fine. The day was just a normal day at work for me. When I left work, I went straight to the flat to meet the landlady. We went through the inventory and read all the meters. She told me I had left the flat in excellent condition and I handed back my two sets of keys. She mentioned that she was surprised I had chosen this day of all days to hand back the keys and she would have understood if I had wanted to choose another day. I told her it had been planned that way on purpose, because it meant that when I woke up the next day I would be starting the second year without Tosh in my own house. The flat was lovely but its rooms had memories of Tosh everywhere. My new house was somewhere he had never been to. So I was beginning the next chapter of my life for me, not us. Once I had handed back the keys I had no time to lose because I would be flying to Las Vegas in six days time.

I had only ever flown to Spain and Dublin on my own before. When I flew to Malaga, Tosh had been at the other end to meet me. When I flew to Dublin, my friends were there to meet the flight. This trip to Las Vegas was going to be very different! I had packed and planned as much as I could, but no amount of planning could prepare me emotionally. Due to the uncertainty of the date of the inquest, I had delayed booking my flight. When I did book it the direct flight had almost doubled in price and had become financially beyond me, so I had to go for an alternative with connections. My flight was from Norwich, my local airport and Mum gave me a lift there. I had it all planned in my mind where the connections were to be and when I needed to check in.

Arriving in good time, I went to check in at the desk in Norwich only to be told I had been put on standby. My flight from Norwich to Amsterdam was fine, but my flight from Amsterdam to Memphis was full and overbooked by six people. They said I could fly to Amsterdam, but until I got there I would not know if I could catch the connecting flight. I asked when the next flight would be, if I was not successful on being picked for the flight and was told the flight was a once a day schedule, so the next flight would not be for another twenty four hours. I was then offered the alternative of being booked on a flight to Chicago. I asked if there was a connecting flight to Las Vegas from there and I was told no. I queried what was to be gained by me flying to Chicago, but she did not have an answer. Already emotionally stretched to my limit with the solo flight coming up and the holiday alone, I just burst into tears. Everyone said how brave it was to be doing this trip alone and many admitted they could not do it. I think I just kept telling myself I would be fine, but now I had hit my first hurdle, I'd gone to pieces.

There was nothing I could do but fly to Amsterdam and just hope I got on the flight. I know Mum was worried about me going all that way alone in the first place and now to see me in sobs of tears must have worried her even more. In the weeks before my trip, I had taught her to text on her mobile phone so she could stay in touch with me to reassure her I was fine. It must have been very difficult to watch her daughter disappear through the departure gate, not knowing when she would get to her final destination of Las Vegas. I went through the gate, passed through the security checks no problem. Once in the departure lounge I heard my flight had been delayed, giving me more to worry about. I opened my book and tried to relax.

Eventually, I boarded the forty five minute flight and arrived safely in Amsterdam. As I was not certain of being put on my connecting flight, I had to collect my suitcase in arrivals instead of it being put straight on the next flight for me. Making my way to check in for the Memphis flight I was told to take a seat. There I sat for about twenty minutes, feeling more and more nervous. I was joined by the other standby passengers and we were all looking at each other, knowing if one of us got on it might mean the others could be stood down. It was a horrible twenty minutes and it felt like hours. Eventually my name was called and I was given a ticket and told to proceed to the departure gate.

I was so relieved. When I was safely through the gate I sent a text to my Mum to let her know the good news and that my plans were back on track. I had arranged to have two hours between each connection, to give me time for delayed flights and toilet stops. I reached Memphis and wandered around the airport taking in the sights and smells. Now I was in America, I thought I would indulge myself in their cuisine, so I bought myself a cheese burger and chips and a cup of coffee. The airport was full of shops and many were selling memorabilia of Elvis, because Memphis was where he had lived when he was not in Las Vegas. His home 'Graceland' was a major tourist attraction and you can even stay in Heartbreak Hotel and tour Sun Studios, where he was first discovered. I only had two hours at the airport and because I was already checked in right through to Las Vegas I could not leave the airport.

So Memphis, Graceland and Sun Studios would have to be another trip sometime in the future. The time passed quickly and I was then boarding the final leg of my journey, on my way to the city of neon! Three and a half hours and I would be there! I got chatting to a couple on the plane, who were going to celebrate their twentieth wedding anniversary and had travelled from Canada. They asked if I was travelling alone and where I was from and I explained I was alone and making the trip to say goodbye to Tosh and they were amazed. I tend to forget that when people find out you are a widow they are first in shock and then disbelief. I had only turned thirty eight a few days before and had been told that the years had been kind to me and I didn't look my age. So the shock that someone like me was too young to be widowed was often very noticeable.

We chatted about Las Vegas and exchanged details of the plans for our trips. They were only staying for five nights, so planning the time was important. There is so much to see and do in this wonderful city. I was staying fourteen nights, so had more time to change things as I went along. As we approached Las Vegas we flew over Hoover Dam, which looked like a little dot down below us. Luck was on my side and, as we descended into McCarran Airport, the lights of the city were shining outside my window to welcome me. The sight of Las Vegas from the air at night is amazing.

I joined the non-US citizen queue and waited to pass through yet more security checks. When my turn came, I had to look into a camera to have my eyes photographed and was then asked to step back for a head and shoulders shot. This was part of the increased security since the attacks on New York's Twin Towers, on September 11th 2001. Having been to America three times, this trip was my fourth since 9/11 so I was not concerned. The security man asked me where I had come from and was surprised I had travelled all that way alone. He asked the purpose of my visit and how long I intended to stay. I answered his questions and he wished me a pleasant stay and hoped that I was able to say my goodbyes and win big on the slot machines. We both laughed, knowing a big win on the slot machines was like the Holy Grail. He said the words that would be repeated time after time during my stay, 'have a nice day', sending me on my way.

## CHAPTER TWENTY TWO

Welcome to Las Vegas. I felt safe, energised and like I had come home. With fourteen nights ahead of me and only me to please, it felt wonderful. I wished my family and friends could have seen this feeling, because it would have eased their worried minds. I strolled through the airport and out to the bus stop.

I bought a ticket to 'The Strip.' My hotel name was taken and I was on my way. I had quickly entered the strange world of tipping and I was in possession of this weird looking money that was all the same size and colour. The only way of distinguishing between notes was to check the numbers. I had two dollars in my sweaty little hand ready to give to the driver, who got my case from the back of the bus when he dropped me at the entrance to The Excalibur Hotel and Casino. He doffed his cap, and told me to 'have a nice day'; thanking him and giving him my two dollar tip I replied 'you too.' I entered the hotel and the noise and lights just hit me, the slot machines were chinking and music was calling you to try your luck. Flashing lights and promises of jackpot wins decorated each machine in an eye-catching display.

The hotels in Las Vegas are all very similar in layout and to reach the hotel check -in, restaurants, cafes, theatres or shops, you have to first pass through the enticing metal machinery. I arrived at around eleven at night and the place was packed with people playing slot machines and table games. It was a Sunday night so the weekenders were enjoying a final flutter before returning home. Not many people were checking in, so I did not have long to wait before I was being checked into the hotel. I was given a non- smoking double room. They don't do singles, so I had a huge room just for me. Check-in was swift and I was soon on my way to find my room. The main hotels in Las Vegas are themed and tourist attractions in their own right. The Excalibur Hotel and Casino is styled as King Arthur's Castle and reminiscent of the days of Camelot. The rooms were based in two towers and the casino was in the centre, with the food outlets and shops dotted around the edge.

My room was in tower two and on the seventeenth floor. I found my way to the elevator and proceeded to track down my room. It was huge - I had a king size bed, table with four chairs, a deep comfortable lounge chair, two bedside tables and the dressing table took up the whole length of one wall! I had an alcove for hanging my clothes and a separate bathroom. The bathroom had a double sink, toilet and one wall was a complete walk in shower. It is very rare to see a bath in Las Vegas hotels, as they use too much water, we are in the middle of the desert after all! This was to be my home for the next fourteen nights. Now the worry of arriving was over, I worked out the time difference and discovered with the delays and transfer to the hotel I had been travelling for twenty three hours since leaving Mum and Dad's house. It was a long time, but well worth the effort.

Several people were worried about me travelling and what kind of emotional state I might be in on arrival and had requested that I text them to reassure that I was safe. The first was to Mum and Dad, the next was to Val and then Edward. He had been in touch a few days before, as he had known the first anniversary had just passed. His life was still confusing (he was in the process of getting divorced), but he said he still wanted to know I was safe. It would be around eight in the morning in England, so I was not sure if anyone would reply but within five minutes Edward had texted back, saying he had been thinking of me and he was glad I was safe and to enjoy myself. Vanessa had been in touch before I had left, but I was not sure of her shifts, and did not want to interrupt her sleep pattern. Also, with the time difference and not being quite sure what day it was, I put her on the postcard list rather than the text lists. Now everyone knew I was fine, I set off to find some food. Restaurants were closed now as it was approaching midnight and the casino was heaving with people.

Excalibur is themed like a castle and attracts families, so I had decided to eat in the twenty four hour coffee shop in the next hotel along the strip. This is the Luxor... as the name suggests this hotel is set in Egypt. The shape of the main body of the hotel is a pyramid. The place was buzzing; I passed slot machines, craps tables, and a huge Poker room full of players, a lounge bar with live music and dancing. It was almost one in the morning but you would not know it. When I got to the café I had to queue and this became my next big test because I was apprehensive about eating out alone. I had picked up a free Poker magazine on my way through the casino, so I had something to read in the café. I need not have worried though, lots of people were on their own. It was like I had been transported to another world. I felt safe, confident, comfortable and, for the first time in over a year, relaxed and happy. I sat eating homemade chicken pie and fries, washed down with fresh coffee. I was able to breathe again and enjoy my favourite hobby of people watching over the top of my coffee cup.

I knew it was not real life, but I was on holiday and I did not have to put on a happy front to anyone, because no-one here knew me. I could just be myself. Who was that person? Who was I? I had never been on holiday alone ever. I would not have had the confidence to do this before, I had rarely travelled outside my 'comfort zone', but I wanted to come to this magical place Tosh and I had enjoyed so much, just to prove to myself I could do it. I had no idea when I set out if I would even like the place and had I only come here before because he liked it? In the next two weeks I would find lots of answers to my unanswered questions. For the moment, at around one thirty am, I was enjoying people watching in the city of neon. Viva Las Vegas!!

I had purposely chosen the same hotel to stay in because it was familiar, if I stayed somewhere else I would not know if I had said my final goodbye to Tosh. I needed to test my feelings. I had arrived on the Sunday night and the first Thursday I was there was a national holiday, it was Thanksgiving. I had made up my mind that I would give the first few days to Tosh and then celebrate Thanksgiving as the start of my new life. I slept well and woke around ten thirty am: my body clock did not know what it was doing. I got showered and dressed and glanced across at my monkey…I expect you're wondering what I mean by that?! In my office we have three cuddly monkeys, they are called 'see no evil', 'hear no evil' and 'speak no evil'. As a team we decided that every time someone went on holiday they would take a monkey with them and photograph the monkey on holiday.

I was very self-conscious of this, as I was on holiday alone, so I decided to take 'see no evil' downstairs with me and take a few photos - then he could relax in the room for the next two weeks. When I got downstairs, I thought of taking his picture with a slot machine but because he had magnets in his feet I didn't know if this would upset the machines. I saw a man and a lady by the roulette table with a clipboard counting the casino chips and checking the table for flaws and damage. I approached the man, explaining about the monkey, and he laughed and said it was not a problem. He asked me what part of England I was from. Most people so far thought I was Australian. I told him I was from Norfolk, he was from Yorkshire and his family were currently living in Great Yarmouth. I was amazed how small the world was. He took the glass off the roulette wheel, for me to take a photograph of the monkey on the roulette table. The lady who was with him thought we were quite mad, but he understood what I needed and directed me to the next photo opportunity, a slot machine with a big jackpot. I then went to the shop and bought a large can of American beer and the monkey and I went back to the room. A photo was taken with the beer and the monkey's duties were complete!

Now free to explore my surroundings, the plan was to revisit the places Tosh and I had visit together. Walking around the Excalibur, I spoke out loud to Tosh to let him know what he was missing. The Poker Room had been moved and was now more than double its original size, as Poker was now big business in Las Vegas. I then wandered onto Las Vegas Boulevard, commonly known as 'The Strip'. I went to the Monte Carlo on my way to my favourite casino on the strip, the Bellagio (the Bellagio is themed on an area of Italy).

The inside was filled with beautiful artwork and decorations and the attention to detail is amazing. The Bellagio was also a favourite place for Tosh to play Poker. I made straight for the Poker room. It was in the same place it had been two years before but, like all the other Poker rooms I had seen so far, it had been extended. It is the most beautifully decorated room, like a stunning museum or a stately home. I expect most of the Poker players do not notice their splendid surroundings. Another big change I noticed is that the Poker rooms are non smoking and Tosh would have loved this as a non smoker.

Having watched the Poker players for a while, I made my way to the check-in area. Next to this area is a giant conservatory, housing living plants. The displays are changed five times a year - Spring, Summer, Autumn (or fall, as they say in the States), Winter and the Chinese New Year. At the moment the display was autumn, the colours were spectacular with the golden colours of the pumpkins and flowers and the burnt oranges of trees and bushes with their leaves changing colour. The centrepiece was a working watermill, giving you an idea of how huge the conservatory is.

The size of the glass domed area is 13,573 square feet. The sun was shining through the glass roof, reminding me it was still daylight, so I made my way outside to continue my day.

The themed hotels in Las Vegas mean you can travel the world without leaving the city. I woke up in King Arthur's castle at the Excalibur, had breakfast in Egypt in The Luxor. I had then been to Monte Carlo and was now visiting Italy with my trip to the Bellagio. I still had the Paris Hotel, Caesar's Palace (Rome), The Mirage (Polynesian Island), The New York New York, The Venetian (Venice), and The Aladdin (Morocco), not to mention The Orleans and The Rio. Some of the names of the hotels obviously give a clue to their themes, while others are just parts of Las Vegas history like The Flamingo, The New Frontier, The Riviera and of course the Las Vegas Hilton.

One of the older hotels had closed its doors the week before I arrived. That was the Stardust. It was opened in 1958 and closed in 2006. It was a hotel I would have liked to have wandered around, as it was the first hotel we stayed in when we first visited Las Vegas in November 2003. It was my fourth trip back and Las Vegas still felt a wonderful place to me. I had shed a tear for Tosh knowing he would have loved the city and the changes I had found, like the enlarged Poker rooms and the fact they were now smoke-free. However, I was starting to realise this was my time. We had visited Hoover Dam together but we never got chance to go to the Grand Canyon. I was determined I was going to take this tour during my trip, as I knew it would be a while before I could return. I wanted to fly over the Grand Canyon at sunset, as I had read the colours were awesome. As it was Thanksgiving week, the flights were getting booked up but I managed to get a plane trip booked.

The company picked me up at my hotel and took me out to Henderson Airfield just half an hour's ride outside Las Vegas. When I arrived I was weighed and was told this was so people of similar weights could be seated to balance the bodies in the small aircraft and was directed to the waiting room. We waited and waited and waited…and were then told there would be a slight delay, as our plane had got a puncture. Trust my luck, at that rate it was going to be dark before we took to the air. Eventually, after being given a free beer we were loaded onto the aircraft. It held only fourteen people and we all had a window seat. We were given headphones for the in-flight commentary and the flight took off. My luck was changing as we flew out over Hoover Dam.

The Dam stood out so clearly and I got some wonderful photographs of the view from my window. We continued out and got to the edge of the Grand Canyon, just as the sun was setting and the colours were breathtaking. The Grand Canyon is two hundred and seventy seven miles long and in places five thousand feet deep, so we only saw the edge of it, but it was a sight I shall never forget. The natural erosion of the rock was incredible. We flew out over the Canyon for about half an hour before the light started to fade and the pilot announced that he would usually head back now… but as we had been delayed he would extend our trip to throw in the bonus of a flight over the strip. It was now about five pm, so the neon was in full glory. As we flew over the Bellagio, as if on cue, the dancing fountains exploded in the lake below. The fountains perform daily every half hour to music. The formation of water reaches heights of two hundred and forty feet in the air. These are floodlit at night and dance in time to the music, which varies from classical to pop. The most moving piece of music I heard was the 'Star Spangled Banner', it would melt the heart of anyone. I could understand how the American citizens felt such pride in their flag and nation when I heard this song playing through the loudspeakers.

As our flight came to a close, we flew over the Mirage Hotel and as we did so their volcano erupted, something that only happens once an hour. The volcano erupts with flames and molten lava (in reality it's piped gas) and is very realistic and warm to stand next to on a chilly night. We were delivered back to our hotels, with wonderful memories of our spectacular flight, I headed to my bed and had an early night. Las Vegas is known for its gambling and its shows. I am only a small gambler, but the live shows are one of my favourite past times. Most people arrive in Las Vegas for only a few days, the average length of stay being four to five days. As I was there for longer, I could pick and choose what show I wanted to see. In previous visits, I had discovered the half price ticket booths. These are places to queue up and buy tickets for the shows for half the normal retail price, the only catch was that you had to stand in line for about half an hour and they were only valid for that night's performance, so it was pot luck what was available. I took full advantage of this offer and saw the following shows:

Mamma Mia, Phantom of the Opera, A Night with Frank Sinatra, Legends in Concert at the Imperial Palace and Jay White.

Today was Thanksgiving Day and I chose on this special holiday to see Jay White. He is the best Neil Diamond if Neil is not around and his show was fantastic. I was surrounded by a very excitable American audience. When he sang 'America', they were on their feet. As the Stars and Stripes flag dropped dramatically behind Jay as he sang, a huge roar from the crowd made a wonderful Thanksgiving celebration. They are so patriotic. This also signalled the start of my new year. I had said my goodbyes and discovered Las Vegas will always hold a special place in my heart and I have found a place where I feel closest to Tosh. He was not at the railway line, or in our flat, or even at his graveside. He was here in Las Vegas and it was time to let him go. I said my goodbyes to him and my time was now!

For the rest of the holiday, I spent time with nine different Elvis Impersonators. The greatest impersonator I had seen during my previous trips was Steve Connolly. Steve was what you could call Elvis in the slim and trim years. He has a wonderful talent and his show gives him a chance to showcase his own music and his wonderful rapport with the audience. He is just like Elvis, but living and breathing and just as sexy.

I drank free double shots of Jack Daniels (this is free if you order drinks whilst gambling). I was only playing five cent machines but the waitresses got to know my order after the third night and from night four to fourteen they just asked if I wanted my usual. The price was simply the one dollar tip. Where in the world can you be served double JD for fifty seven pence? Viva Las Vegas!! I spent five hours in the Elvis Museum and visited the Auto Collection at the Imperial Palace Hotel. I went to the movies in the Orleans Hotel and ate buttered popcorn watching Hugh Grant bumble his way across the screen, who could ask for more? I also shopped in the Thanksgiving sales, making the most of some seasonal bargains.

I love Las Vegas and the only factors stalling my return are the long journey to America and the finances!

# CHAPTER TWENTY THREE

Since Tosh's death in November 2005 my world has completely changed. Living with someone for so many years, you become familiar with their personality and their habits. When Tosh died suddenly, that person was no longer around. He was the stability in my life and after he died I was left to pick up the pieces, still trying to take care of myself, learning the skills and tasks he had taken on in our relationship. We had some fantastic times together, but we also had some rough times too. He would be the first to admit he was very hard to live with, but we adjusted to each other and despite everything we loved each other to the end and beyond. He always said I needed to come out of my comfort zone more often and I can say without a doubt that I have moved out of that zone entirely.

At the time Tosh died my confidence was at an all time low. I could not even make a decision on what brand of beans to buy, for fear of buying the wrong brand. All that had now changed. I was forced to make so many decisions and choices in my daily life that I had only one way to go. I'm certain many people will say my insecurities were my own doing and I am sure lots of people cannot imagine being so controlled by someone they love so much, that they don't want to speak up for themselves. I now feel liberated and free. Yes, I am making mistakes and if I get it wrong the world will not fall in and lightning bolts will not strike the ground before me. If I make a mistake, I try to correct it and learn not to do the same thing wrong next time. Sometimes I remember and sometimes I don't.

When Tosh died, I was thrown into the unfamiliar territory of loneliness, sadness and grief. I was feeling so many different emotions - firstly of shock and disbelief that this had happened, then I then had to deal with the loss of someone so important in my life, losing his love, his friendship, the companionship and the intimacy we shared.

Not only had I lost Tosh, but the only person I could share past memories with. No one else can share the things we had lived through. Who would remember our trips to Ireland, to the greyhound sales, or remember his greyhound 'Rich Son'?

Who will remember the moment our septic tank got a puncture and had to be dug out? Or the time when his fear of hospitals, opticians and dentists raised its head? He would regularly blackout at the opticians and when visiting the dentist he would have to wait outside in the bus shelter until his turn was called. When I had my two front teeth removed he blacked out on the pavement outside, even though there was no visible sign of blood or pain. The dentist had to bring him round with smelling salts and was surprised to see him in this state, as he had not been in the building (he had been in the bus shelter) or had any treatment that day! Who will remember the relief when we sold the house in Spain, or the heartache we had when making the decision that brought us back to England? Who will be able to share the memory of him sitting at a Poker table in Binions Horseshoe, Las Vegas, for the preliminary rounds of the World Series of Poker and the joy on his face as he was playing and beating the professionals around the table at that event? So many joint memories are wiped when you lose the only other person who was there to share them.

Another emotion I am not proud of is envy. Everyone seems to be in a couple, or have someone when you are now so alone. The hardest thing for me is when someone says without thinking that they were having an argument with their husband or wife and they feel life would be better if they were on their own. That makes me so angry. I know I should hold my tongue, but sometimes I fail and tell them what I think. Being alone is not as wonderful as you think. The novelty of watching what you want on television, playing the music you like at a volume of choice and eating your favourite food when you want, wears off pretty quickly. If having someone to share my life with again means watching sport from time to time, it's a sacrifice I would be prepared to make.

For anyone who has not experienced the journey of grief through bereavement, the best way for me to explain it to you is to compare it to walking along a rocky road. You begin slowly and cautiously, only at a pace that your confidence and emotions will allow. You pick up a bit of speed. Then suddenly, without warning, you will lose your footing and stumble badly. During the grieving process the bereaved person will begin to heal and will start to have days where they won't cry as much, or will have slept for a few hours, or even feel like eating again. Then suddenly, without warning and sometimes without reason, they will hit a bump in the recovery process. They will cry and sob and be unable to sleep again. Gradually, these bumps smooth out and the journey becomes bearable. There is no set time or length for this recovery and it cannot be bypassed. It just has to take it heart-wrenching course.

When you begin to come out of the other side of your grief, you will often look back on your past life. I have looked back and wondered, if I had the chance to go back and relive this life we shared, knowing what I know about the pain and hurt that has been caused to the families and myself, would I do the same again?

The answer would be 'yes', I would do it all again. I regret the hurt I have caused the families, but I had lived a full and happy life with Tosh. I had some scary, lonely times and I should have stood up to his dominant personality, but sharing my life with him has made me into the person I am today. No-one is perfect, I know Tosh had his faults, but he loved me and I know people can go through their whole lives without having that feeling, so I feel very lucky.

I have had the added pressure of being reunited with two families. Not everyone has welcomed me back with open arms, but what did I expect? I know I have hurt my family badly in the past and I am now cautious of hurting them again. They have been through enough! The love I have been given from my parents, my sister Kath and her husband Peter is amazing. I am equally surprised that I have been made a part of Tosh's family. I have been hugged and loved by Marlene and Bramwell and their family and included in their family gatherings. They have treated me as one of their own. All those that are happy to have me back in their lives have told me and shown me in so many different ways. I hope they know how much they mean to me. I am still learning about relationships and will make many mistakes and I just hope my family and friends will help me learn how to be a part of their lives in the future.

One thing I have noticed is how many people now greet me with a hug and a kiss. It makes me feel loved and wanted, whether it's Mum or Dad, Marlene and Bramwell, Kath, Pete, Dan, Val or Vanessa. That physical contact tells a person so much. I thank them for being so open with their hugs and kisses and long may they continue!

I was so lucky when Vanessa was sent to my door that day. The moment we met, our personalities clicked immediately. I felt safe, comfortable and had no fear of asking her anything. She was so compassionate and only a year older than my thirty seven years on that first meeting. She was psychologically years older than me, through life experience gained by the things she sees on a daily basis, in her job as a policewoman. The more time I spent with Vanessa, I came to realise what an exceptional human being she is. The hours and shifts she works are crazy - twelve hour shifts, four days on and four days off, with days off cancelled at the last minute. However, as an FLO, her phone could ring at anytime, even on an off duty day. I thought of Vanessa as more of a friend, we had laughed together and cried together. Our sense of humour was similar and I felt at ease with her.

Thankfully I was proven right and we have become friends. We no longer contact each other on the 24/7 phone and the trust that had built between us during her professional support has spilled over into friendship. We can now contact each other if we are having a good day or bad day, as friends do. Due to our busy lives we can go for great periods of time when we don't see each other or speak on the phone, but when we are in contact again it's like we have spoken or seen each other only moments before. I have discovered the caring, considerate Vanessa is the real Vanessa and not just part of the job, as she is the same person when she is off duty. I feel very lucky to have her as a friend. Our friendship and trust has meant she has felt able to contact me when she has had a rough time in her life and needed a friend. It works both ways now, which is a much better feeling.

Val has been a constant friend in my life for so many years and I don't know how I will ever repay her kindness and friendship. She has helped me and been my emotional support even when Tosh was alive. When I was asked by the policeman that fateful day if there was a friend you can call, because he had some bad news, I didn't hesitate to dial her number. Val had held me when I needed a hug, or needed a cry and also laughed with me when I needed to laugh. Friends like Val are a rare breed and I am extremely lucky to know her and have her as my friend. She has welcomed me into her family. Val has been my best friend, mum, sister, aunt and confidant for so long. I can tell her anything and she does not judge me, she knows more about me than I do sometimes. She has been there for me through good times and bad. I was very wary how my Mum would feel meeting Val for the first time, but I need not have worried. They both hugged each other and have got on really well. I just hope I can be there for Val as she was for me, if the need arises, and I hope I don't let her down.

Mum and Dad have been wonderful. We have become closer than we have ever been. It is sometimes strange when Mum talks of family, or friends and I don't know them, as they have appeared in the time I have been away from the family. I often have to say 'Mum, I'm sorry, I don't know these people' or 'I can't remember this or that happening.' I can compare this to like being in a coma: I have woken up and the world has continued around me. In time I will remember more people, but missed birthdays, weddings and celebrations can never be replaced. They are one off occasions, no amount of video or film will replace these events. You had to be there to share the moments and experience the atmosphere at the time.

One thing that shows they still worry about me is if we have been out, or I have been to Mum and Dad's after dark and I have to go home to an empty house alone. Then I have to give them three rings to let them know I am safe. This means telephoning them and letting the phone ring three times and hanging up. Sometimes Dad forgets and answers it and I have to explain 'this is me giving you three rings, but you picked it up on the second ring!' Other friends and family have adopted this way of communicating that I am home safe. It is just another way of showing they care! I am very lucky to have a second chance.

Dad has helped me a great deal and with his experience and specialist knowledge we have laid a patio. I am filling the space with plants and flowers, my first tomatoes and strawberries tasted so good. Spending time in my home and garden entertaining family and friends was a scary experience to begin with, but I am overcoming the panic attacks and enjoying sharing my time with those I care for.

If someone had told me the actions of someone I loved and cared for would change my life forever I would never believed them. Since Tosh's death I have cried too much, drunk too much, been angry and hurt. When people say their heart feels like it is breaking I know what this feels like. The pain that runs through your body and mind cannot be quantified. I felt helpless at the thought that my love for Tosh was not enough to save him from his inner pain. Regarding the circumstances of what happened, I have become very knowledgeable about half barrier crossings - and I am still of the opinion that they are safe if used correctly.

On a more practical note, I can now use a washing machine and an iron! I inherited a tool box and enough tools to rewire a house, but I have not needed to go quite that far yet. I have become very good at DIY and one of my first projects was to install two roller blinds and they do manage to roll up and down! I am so proud of myself and have given every visitor a demonstration of the blinds going up and down when they first tour my new home. I have become very skilled at the art of flat pack furniture assembly too and am now the proud owner of a full set of Allan keys.

My new home has been decorated by my own fair hands too. I have chosen and laid a new floor covering in my bathroom and kitchen and painted the majority of the house in my own choice of colour scheme. It makes a change to transform a house into a home and I have no immediate plans to sell and move on. I now have more furniture than Tosh or I ever thought of owning, though it is still sparsely furnished to some people's taste. I have enjoyed choosing bargains that make my home look like it is decorated with more expensive products, I have a few photos and candles around the place, although my home is still largely clutter free. If I buy something and it does not fit in or does not have a practical use, it is usually passed on to friends or family, or a charity shop!

I am gradually overcoming my panic attacks and am now more comfortable with entertaining. My speciality in the kitchen is Shepherd's Pie. Everyone who has been invited to eat at my table has been served this signature dish at some point.

Being bereaved suddenly at the age of thirty seven has given me so much life experience I never intended to want or need. The work with the suicide widows with Jacqui continues. We never anticipated such a need for us to share our experiences, but suicide is a growing problem and widows both male and female are joining us for cyber support.

I have come to realise that there is a need for bereavement support at a local level for those in a similar position and I am currently pursuing avenues in which I may be able help others. Being a widow is no longer just for people in their seventies. The pain and loss is the same whatever your age or sex, but the shock and the hurdles a young widow has to face and overcome are not always the same as our older counterparts. I have no idea how I would have got this far without friendship, support and love from others. If I can help others who are travelling this terrible journey, then my sadness and pain would not have been in vain.

I still have some way to go to reach the life I am comfortable with. My sad days are less as time moves on. I still find it hard not having someone to hold me and love me and ask at the end of the day 'how was your day dear?'

I need to gain the confidence to go out and make new friends, but I have come so far since my life changing moment on the thirteenth of November 2005.

Writing my story has been an emotional journey. What started out as a few thoughts on my life with Tosh, to help our families fill in the missing years we were apart, has extended to share some of the pain and struggles I have faced in adjusting to my new 'normal' way of living. If my words and ramblings have helped just one person to feel they are not alone in the life they are living, then my pain would have been worthwhile.

Two years after Tosh's death I still suffer from panic attacks, though very few people would notice as I've learnt to hide it extremely well. I also suffer from feelings of not being worthy of love and friendship from time to time.

I am struggling to find ways of making new friends of my own age. Living with no friends for so long, I forgot the social skills of how to find friends and, once they have been found, how to keep them. I have to learn the guidelines of when to be in contact and also when to back off, so I don't end up being viewed as some kind of stalker!

I have gained confidence but this is an ongoing struggle. I still yearn for someone to share my life with and, as I approach my fortieth birthday, I have hope that my life will truly begin again!